Energetic Meetings

Enhancing Personal and Group Energy

&

Handling Difficult Behavior

Jeanie Marshall

Jemel Publishing House
P.O. Box 977
Santa Monica. CA 90406-0977

Energetic Meetings
Enhancing Personal and Group Energy & Handling Difficult Behavior

Published by

Jemel Publishing House
P.O. Box 977
Santa Monica, CA 90406-0977

Copyright © 1994 by Jeanie Marshall
Incorporating *Handling Difficult Behavior at Meetings* © 1982, 1984, 1994
Cover design and illustration by Lightbourne Images Copyright © 1994
Printed in the United States of America.

PUBLISHER'S NOTE
This publication is designed to provide helpful suggestions with respect to the subject matter covered. It is sold with the understanding that the publisher is not engaged in rendering psychological, medical, or other professional services. If expert assistance or counseling is needed, the services of a competent professional are recommended.

ORDERING INFORMATION
To order, call toll-free 1-800-460-5855. For corporate volume discounts or bookstore inquiries, call (310) 458-1172. See additional ordering information on back page.

Library of Congress Catalog Card Number: 94-096350
Marshall, Jeanie
ENERGETIC MEETINGS: *Enhancing Personal and Group Energy & Handling Difficult Behavior*

ISBN 1-885893-00-0

About the Author

Jeanie Marshall, Empowerment Consultant, is founder and president of Marshall House. Her M.S. is in Human Resource Development from The American University and NTL Institute. She produces and hosts a local television show entitled, *Return to Center.*

In *Energetic Meetings*, Jeanie offers insights and suggestions from eighteen years in the field of individual, group, and organizational development. She blends traditional approaches with innovative ideas to stimulate creativity and effectiveness at meetings. Her deep and profound understanding of personal and group energy accelerates lasting transformation.

Publications include:

"Trainer Type Inventory"
University Associates *1986 Annual: Developing Human Resources*

Dealing with Difficult Behavior
Assertiveness for Career and Personal Success
American Management Association

Handling Difficult Behavior at Meetings
A booklet published by Marshall House

Thirty two audio cassette tapes
for relaxation, meditation, and information

Monthly subscription newsletter
Marshall House Journal

Forthcoming books:

The Symbolic Language of Energy
Affirmations: A Pathway to Empowerment
A transformational novel

Marshall House
P.O. Box 918
Santa Monica, CA 90406

Telephone (310) 458-1172
Fax (310) 451-2265
Voice Mail (310) 558-6857

Acknowledgements

We appreciate the helpful feedback and supportive encouragement from the following individuals, all of whom are competent professionals in their own field.

Bonnie Hutchinson
Hutchinson Associates, Edmonton, Alberta, Canada

Ozzie Bermant
The Concordia Systems Group, Potomac, Maryland

Sharon Matthias, M.Sc., M.B.A.
Sharon J. Matthias Consulting, Ltd., Edmonton, Alberta, Canada

Jeff Hutner
Jeff Hutner Consulting, Ojai, California

Crystal Cheryl Bell, RSc.P., CPS
LifeSource Ministries, Santa Monica, California

Kerimera Sseruwamikisa
Sserulanda Foundation, Los Angeles and Uganda

Donna Himot, M.B.A.
Business Specialties, Los Angeles, California

Jane Bolton, M.A.
Transformational Therapies, Santa Monica, California

Energetic Meetings

Enhancing Personal and Group Energy
&
Handling Difficult Behavior

*is affectionately dedicated to
all persons I have encountered in groups,
especially those who model empowering behavior
and those who act out difficult behavior.*

Table of Contents

Introducing this Book

Dear Reader,

    Thank you for joining me on this adventure. I know that you are busy, so I have created a book that is compact and easy to read. Chapter 1 lays a foundation for the rest of the book. Chapter 2 helps you to find specific ideas in the book.

    As you work with the ideas in *Energetic Meetings*, please share your experiences with me. Future revisions will be inspired by reader input.

                   With Warm Regards,

Jeanie Marshall

                   Jeanie Marshall
                   Empowerment Consultant

Chapter 1

Dear Reader

Celebrating The Birth of this Book; The Birth of a Nation

In July of 1976, I stormed out of a meeting in disgust and anger. I felt frustrated and disempowered. I said to myself emphatically, "I'm never going to another meeting!"

Never is a long time! I soon rescinded this vow.

The energy burst of feelings about that meeting's ineffectiveness and my wasted time were soon channeled in constructive ways. I allowed my passion for finding and creating meaning to guide me to a variety of experiences.

That event was the birth of my interest in groups that led to the precursor of this book, *Handling Difficult Behavior at Meetings*. That event happened in the month of the Bicentennial celebration of the United States of America. Two hundred years before, the U.S. was born.

It is so often true that out of the depths of anger or loneliness or despair or pain or frustration we find the strength or wisdom to make our most meaningful choices or contributions. Nations, organizations, books, entrepreneurial ventures, and consulting practices often have such beginnings.

The Paths and Windows of Life

My path has led me from meeting to meeting, from group to group, from client organization to client organization. This is the path of an independent consultant. Every situation has whispered or spoken or sung or shouted its gift to me. Every person I have encountered has taught me. Through both pain and joy I have grown so that I can share insights, techniques, principles, strategies, and experiences.

I am delighted that my path has crossed with yours.

I honor that you also have a path on which you have walked. Perhaps you have even stumbled at times. I know I have. Our paths may be similar or quite different. In order to grow and develop, we review or even redirect our path from time to time.

On our paths, we have created windows through which we see our experiences. These windows -- or models or world views or paradigms -- can help us to understand the complexities of the world and solve the problems we encounter. In order to grow and develop, we clean or open the windows. Sometimes we must break them.

The Book's Intention and the Author's Approach

My intention is that *Energetic Meetings* inspires you or provokes your thinking or leads you to see the world in ways that bring you deeper meaning. My intention is that something changes to make your life better as a result of being with me through these pages. Agreeing with all the ideas in *Energetic Meetings* is not required.

Here is a simple window through which I see my work as an empowerment consultant and writer: I encourage you to identify where you are (*the current condition or situation*) and where you want to be (*the desired condition or situation*). If these are the same place, I support you by helping you to enhance or maintain your condition or situation. If your current and desired situations are different, I support you by assisting you in moving from where you are to where you want to be.

Here is an example. Jack called me the other day to tell me that he felt attacked in his senior management meeting that morning. I have worked with Jack for three years and have found him to be a well-respected manager and a consistent contributor to his corporation.

The senior management group includes Jack's six peers and the Vice President to whom they all report. He described the facts of his morning meeting, which I summarize as follows:

His current condition or situation: He feels attacked because he made a factual mistake, resulting in deeper feelings of inadequacy and fear of credibility loss.

His desired condition or situation: He wants to be respected, feel good about himself, and be able to make a mistake without being humiliated.

Jack began to analyze his own situation, which is characteristic of people who want to grow. He started to talk about what he could do differently or what he felt he should do differently.

"For one thing, I should've had my facts straight. That's how this all started." Jack said, feeling remorse and guilt.

I heard what Jack was saying on many different levels. Often when individuals use the word "should," they show an energy pattern that we might describe as "devitalized." Judgments, such as this one that Jack made about himself, indicate feelings of guilt and remorse. *Shoulds* tend to lower self esteem and deplete personal energy.

I spoke first to the feelings, and then to the facts. "Jack, you obviously feel bad that you made a mistake. You may want to take back the error. But, guess what?! You'll probably make an error sometime again. You can't protect yourself from the world by never making another mistake."

"I suppose not," Jack said thoughtfully.

"Remember, too, that because of this so-called error, you now have an opportunity to learn deeply about yourself and others what you wouldn't have learned if all your numbers had been correct."

"Hmm," came the sound from the other end of the telephone. He recognized that the pain of the morning meeting was leading to something greater. He was ready to look below the pain.

I continued, "I see a much deeper issue here." And then I probed, "What's the deeper issue for *you*?"

"That I can't get upset at every little error."

I both agreed and disagreed. Verbally I said, "Mistakes *do* happen. When we let ourselves learn from them, they're gifts. An error-free life is not necessarily a meaningful one. Personally, if I had not made many mistakes I wouldn't be as successful as I am."

"That's a helpful way of looking at mistakes. Is there another deeper issue *you* see in this?" Jack took his turn to ask me a probing question.

"I feel you've touched on the deeper issue. Let me just expand on it. I see one of the deeper issues as the group's relationship to mistakes. Or, as you like to say, the "cultural norms" about mistakes and how they're handled. This group, of course, includes *you*."

"Come to think of it, that *is* the deeper issue, isn't it? I've mocked others when *they've* made mistakes. Just last week I said to one of my peers "Stupid mistake, Dave, really stupid." I remember I was thinking, *he's strong, he can take this*. He already felt bad. I just made him feel worse. I guess I deserve what I got today."

"Jack, let the cycle stop here. This is not about retaliation or punishment, but an experience that can teach you. When you understand that a pattern is locked into the organization, or, as I like to say, 'in the energy field,' you can break the pattern."

"But I'm only one person. Just because I might stop chiding someone doesn't mean others will stop."

"Be careful you don't get caught in the 'I'm-only-one-person' syndrome, Jack. It's a path to apathy. It may be true that you don't see changes initially in others just because you break a personal pattern. It isn't up to you to get others to change, anyway. If only for your *own* sake, it's worthwhile to see mistakes differently -- to see people differently."

Jack's energy had shifted. I could *feel* it over the telephone, even though nearly three thousand miles separated us physically. So, I decided to continue, "People are very important. Each person has a gift to bring to the organization. An organization exists *only* because of people. We all want to be respected, to be empowered, to feel good, to know that we make a positive difference."

Jack summarized our conversation most succinctly when he said, "I know that I don't have to dwell on this event. I can use it to make a difference in my life and organization. My new intention is to use each situation to empower myself and others. I want others to feel better because they've had an encounter with me."

When others in Jack's organization explore the results of their actions, without blaming themselves or others; they, too, will come to similar conclusions. The painful and destructive interactions in groups, organizations, families -- all relationships -- can stop instantly if we change our beliefs from competition to collaboration, from lack to abundance, from struggle to freedom, from control to empowerment.

When we see the world through a window of collaboration, we tend to ask ourselves and others, "How can we collaborate here?" Feel the difference between that question and, say, "How can I be better than her or him?" The window of empowerment shows us a world of abundance and wholeness that operates with divine power rather than "power over" which emanates from a belief in separation and scarcity.

Energetic Meetings is about creating group meetings and all other encounters that are energetic, meaningful, enriching, and empowering. I challenge you: **Leave every meeting empowered!** When you leave a meeting -- solo or with the rest of the participants -- let it be an act of or toward empowerment for you and everyone else.

Energy, Energy Field, Energetics

In this book, I use the following words and phrases interchangeably: energy, energy field(s), and energetics. My underlying belief -- my window -- is that the whole universe is composed of energy. Every person and every thing -- each having its own vibration -- is a part of a whole, interconnected by a field of energy which is invisible to ordinary eyesight.

This field of energy contains information that is available to all who will perceive it. Memories of all our experiences are coded in the energy field. The energy field contains sounds inaudible to the physical ear, visions unseen by the physical eyes, and textures untouched by the physical body. Though intangible, the energy field is quite real. As we open to the mystery of it, our world expands. Or some might say, we find a "new" world.

Recognition of the energy field requires trust and/or skill. If you want to understand more deeply about the energy field, simply start where you are. Put down this book, close your eyes, tune out any environmental noises, and simply experience the space in which you find yourself. If you do this several times through your regular day, you will become more sensitive to energy and will find your own ways of experiencing the energy field. Consciousness is the key.

As you gain experience in noticing the energy field, you may find that sometimes it is comfortable and sometimes it is uncomfortable. You can learn to change the energy from uncomfortable or dense or thick or dark to a more comfortable energy. Comfortable energy may feel light or more breathable or sparkling or free.

Energetic Meetings will assist you in discerning and shifting energy. Energy (or the energy field) can be shifted with human intention and expectations. Even our *awareness* of the energy field can begin a shift. The higher our intention and the greater our awareness, the more profound the transformation.

Kinds of Meetings

Energetic Meetings is written to assist you at different kinds of meetings in a variety of settings. The types of meetings include, but are not limited to, groups that gather to solve problems, make decisions, set policy, hear reports, deliver directives, train in new procedures, develop new skills, share information, make proposals, market services.

These gatherings may be known as staff meetings, management meetings, workshops, performance evaluation sessions, public forums, quality circles, committee meetings, training programs, boards, networking sessions, political gatherings, town meetings, or family pow-wows.

The setting for your meetings may be in your work place, community, religious group, or home. It only takes two persons to have a "meeting."

History of the Book's Editions

This is the first edition of *Energetic Meetings: Enhancing Personal and Group Energy & Handling Difficult Behavior.* It includes the third edition of *Handling Difficult Behavior at Meetings,* a booklet which is also available separately.

The first edition of *Handling Difficult Behavior at Meetings* was written in 1982 as a compilation of many ideas generated at training programs which I designed and facilitated. This first edition of *Energetic Meetings* includes an updated version of *Handling Difficult Behavior at Meetings* and incorporates ideas about the empowering use of personal, group, and organizational energy.

Chapter 2

Finding
What You Want
in
This
Book

Reading and Using this Book

Energetic Meetings is written especially for consultants, trainers, managers, group leaders, and meeting participants. If you do not fall neatly into one or more of these categories, yet are drawn to read this book, *Energetic Meetings* is also written for you.

This book is organized into three content sections in addition to this introductory section: Creating a Climate of Positive Energy, Generating Positive Contributions, and Handling Difficult Behavior. A final section lists suggested books for further reading.

I have attempted to make the book's style one that is easy to read now and to refer to later, as needed. I recognize that readers have different needs and interests. While my ego wants you to read and savor every word, I prefer that you benefit from those parts that attract you and not be distracted by those parts that do not interest you. Parts that do not interest you now may interest you later. They will be waiting for you.

Ozzie Bermant, founder of The Concordia Systems Group in Potomac, Maryland, says, "There is so much in *Energetic Meetings* that will be appealing to anyone -- new age, middle age, and old age folks." In an effort to help you to locate those parts that are most interesting to you, I have selected several themes and references. A chapter-by-chapter summary follows these references.

Themes, Scenarios, and Chapter References

Here are some of the themes covered in *Energetic Meetings* and the chapters in which they appear. For some subjects, additional insights are also included. As you find parts of the book that are particularly relevant for you, you may want to add those references to this chapter.

THEME: ENERGY, ENERGETICS, ENERGY FIELD

You feel skeptical about the concept of "energy" or "energy field" or "energetics"......

- Read Chapter 3, especially the segment on "openness." Explore.

You know that intention is powerful and want to understand this concept with respect to energy and groups and meetings......

- Read Chapter 3, especially page 28.

You want to enhance your awareness and experience of energy......

- Practice the simple technique suggested on page 8.
- Read Chapter 3 and practice the concept explained on page 25; also give special attention to page 30.
- Read Chapter 8.
- Set an intention to enhance your awareness and experience of energy.

You want to understand the impact of "energy" on groups......

- Reread the brief description of "energy" in Chapter 1 and practice the simple technique suggested on page 8.
- Read Chapters 3 (especially page 30), 6, and 8.

You want to understand energy with respect to a specific difficult behavior......

- Read Chapters 9 and 10.
- Find the specific behavior that challenges you and read the suggestions listed in Chapter 10.

You want to practice energy work......

- Read Chapter 3, especially the **Marshall Model for Transforming Energy**.
- Apply the techniques that are discussed in Chapter 8.
- Keep a journal of your experiences with the principles and techniques discussed in this book.

THEMES: GROUP DYNAMICS AND MEETING MECHANICS

You are a new or experienced group leader or participant and want to understand more about groups as a dynamic expression.....

- Read Chapter 4, especially about group development, beginning on page 36.

You are a group leader and want a few basic procedures and processes to organize your group meetings for success......

- Read Chapters 4 and 7.

You need help analyzing the various elements of your meeting......

    •Read Chapter 7, pages 73 and following.

You have just left a meeting which you found to be dysfunctional and unsatisfying......

- Read Chapter 4, especially the initial parts.

- Read Chapter 9. Read appropriate parts of Chapter 10 if the dysfunction and/or dissatisfaction seem related to difficult behavior.

You must plan a large meeting and do not know where to start......

- Read Chapter 5.

You are a trainer or meeting facilitator and want techniques for stimulating active participation......

- Read Chapter 6, especially beginning page 61.

- Set a high intention that participants be empowered and actively involved in all aspects of the meeting for the highest good of all concerned.

You want suggestions on establishing ground rules......

- Read Chapter 4 (especially pages 34 and 35).

- Read Chapter 7 (especially page 66 and following).

You want a checklist for enhancing effectiveness before, during, and after your meetings......

- Refer to the checklist in Chapter 5, beginning on page 51.

THEME: EMPOWERMENT

You want a definition of the "empowered person"......

- Read Chapter 6, especially page 58; also page 57.

You want a description of the energetics of empowerment......

- Read Chapter 6.

You want questions you can ask yourself and/or others to encourage greater empowerment......

- Read Chapter 6, especially page 60.

THEME: DIFFICULT BEHAVIOR

You want to understand difficult behavior generally......

- Read Chapter 9.
- Read the summaries of the four categories of difficult behavior patterns (pages 101, 108, 114, and 122).

You are confronted by a specific difficult behavior......

- Turn to the list of twenty-two difficult behavior patterns in Chapter 10 and from there, read about the specific behavior.

You know that your own behavior sometimes challenges others. You want to understand what others face and how they can assist you in being more constructive......

- Identify the difficult behavior pattern and other related behavior patterns in the list on page 100. As you read, love yourself for wanting to develop and expand your awareness of yourself.

Chapter-by-chapter Summary

CREATING A CLIMATE OF POSITIVE ENERGY

This section prompts you to consider ways in which to establish an environment that fosters creativity and success at your meetings. It focuses on both the people and the process with the intention of enhancing communication and participation.

Chapter 3, Energy and Energy Transformation, expands the Chapter 1 definition of energy and energetics. This chapter helps you to consider relevant aspects in your own meetings in order to raise your awareness about this dynamic we call "energy." Guidelines for clearing uncomfortable energetics are described.

Four elements for the empowering use of energy create *The Marshall Model for Transforming Energy*: Intention, Attention, Energy, and Mystery. Questions listed for each of the four elements assist you in applying the principles of the model to your meetings.

Chapter 4, Group Needs and Dynamics, suggests ways to organize your meeting for minimal difficulty and maximum satisfaction. Simple strategies blended with common sense and kindness can be a magical combination in any group.

A model of group development emphasizes the stages that groups experience: forming, storming, norming, and performing. This discussion assists you in supporting a group through its developmental stages. A brief description of the new meeting paradigm opens you to possibilities of deeper satisfaction through group meeting experiences.

Chapter 5, Meeting Arrangements, assists you in arranging for your meeting place and organizing for a successful meeting. A checklist provides you with a list of considerations which you can refer to or check off to help you to create effective meetings.

GENERATING POSITIVE CONTRIBUTIONS

This section includes a myriad of ideas for assisting participants to be actively involved in meaningful ways. These techniques and processes build a foundation for personal and group empowerment.

Chapter 6, Empowered Persons at Meetings, discusses what it means to be "empowered" and the energetics of empowerment. It lists empowering questions that you can ask yourself or others. Active participation enhances satisfaction and improves results.

Chapter 7, Meeting Mechanics, discusses several ideas related to the mechanical aspects of groups. It differentiates between content and process, and focuses on several processes for meeting effectiveness. These include five decision-making methods, ground rules, centering, buzz groups, and brainstorming. The chapter ends with ideas for keeping groups on target and analyzing a meeting.

HANDLING DIFFICULT BEHAVIOR

The intention of the previous two sections is to establish a climate that is so conducive to creativity and affiliation that this section is not needed. But just in case, here are some valuable ideas.

Chapter 8, Energetic Release, focuses on principles and techniques for releasing toxicity from the energy field. It explains how we create energetic toxic waste and how we can dispose of and recycle it properly. Powerful tools are described for you to work with to assist in the transformation of the energetics of your group.

Chapter 9, Difficult Behavior, admits that not everyone agrees about what behavior is "difficult." Your own subjective experiences are important resources in determining what is difficult for you. A matrix of questions guides you into considering the costs and benefits of a conflict situation. As you respond to the questions, you can determine a considerable amount of information that allows you to clarify the appropriate next steps in a conflict situation.

Chapter 10, Twenty-two Difficult Behavior Patterns, outlines behavior that is considered difficult for many leaders or participants at meetings. For each of the twenty-two difficult behavior patterns, one column lists several possible reasons that the person is exhibiting a behavior. (Oh, by the way, "the person" may be you!) Another column lists several possible actions to neutralize the behavior, enhance creativity, build healthy relationships, and/or promote harmony in the group.

Chapter 11, Transforming Difficulty into Empowerment, shifts the window of seeing life as a struggle into seeing every situation as an opportunity for empowerment. This chapter helps to make every difficulty that we have encountered be worthwhile as a learning adventure. It encapsulates the New Meeting Paradigm.

BOOKS FOR FURTHER READING

This final section lists suggested books in several relevant categories.

Creating a Climate of Positive Energy

Energetic, positive, exciting meetings do not just happen "by accident." They result from the clear intention of at least one person in the group. Principles of group dynamics, energetics, and empowerment all assist in the development of meetings that are meaningful and satisfying.

"Positive" and "negative" are subjective terms when applied to a meeting's climate. A synonymous duality is "light and heavy." We might all agree generally to some of the following ideas.

"Negative energy" means the climate is heavy, dense, muddy, or blocked. We may experience a wide range of symptoms or effects. Physically, we may experience illness or fatigue or lethargy. Emotionally, we may feel competitive, angry, or afraid. Or we may experience confusing or disappointing relationships. Mentally, we may tell ourselves we are inferior or believe we are victims. Spiritually, we may feel isolated or without a clear life mission.

"Positive energy" means the energetics are clear, light, or comfortable. Decisions are easier to make. Abundance flows in our ideas and relationships. Actions that benefit humanity come from high intention and empowering thoughts. We experience freedom, collaboration, understanding, synergy, belonging, love, satisfaction, connectedness, meaning, and wisdom.

This section alerts you to elements to consider in starting a group, arranging meeting space, organizing meaningful events and experiences, and focusing on energy and energetics.

Chapter 3

Energy
and
Energy Transformation

Energy, Energetics, Energy Field

For me, everything is energy. Energy vibrates at different rates to produce chairs and persons and emotions and the earth. Everything.

The word "energetics" refers to both the physical and non-physical aspects of persons, places, and things -- and the thoughts that form them. "Energy field" is another term for "energetics." Energy can be perceived physically; that is, by seeing, feeling, hearing, or sensing the resonance -- rough or smooth, green or pink, near or far, hot or cold, etc. Energy can also be perceived non-physically; that is, intuitively or by inner sensing or knowing.

We are quite familiar with the invisible world, although some individuals say they are unfamiliar or wary of anything they cannot touch or see. Here are just a few intangibles we deal with daily: love, distrust, principles, fairness, honesty, integrity, goodwill, uncertainty.

If you argue, "But I can see love and principles" etc., I say no, we can see the *manifestations* of love and hope and joy but we do not see them. As our consciousness expands, we come to rely more on the unseen or intangible aspects of life than the tangible.

Energy at Meetings

A meeting may be on-purpose or off-purpose: either state can be sensed or intuited energetically. Few facts are required when the energy field is tapped for information. Sensitivity to energy gives information about how/where energy is blocked, how/where energetic protective shields are torn, how/where energy is too dense, how/where energy is vibrating at a frequency that disempowers an individual or a group.

Often the introduction of an individual who has this type of awareness can shift the energy so that it flows more appropriately. Other times, more overt tinkering is required. Energy shifts happen with intention and consciousness. Not everyone in the group needs to have the intention or the consciousness in order to make a shift.

How is the energy in *your* group? Is it dense, toxic, confusing? Or light, clear, exciting? Are group members under stress or often ill? Or are group members lively and ready to contribute? Are there miscommunications? Or are communications clear? Are individuals disempowered? Or are they empowered?

Confusion, stress, illness, miscommunications, and disempowerment are indications or symptoms of a problem. Such indications or symptoms tend to create patterns which can lead to deeper understanding of a group.

The individuals and other components of your group comprise the group's whole. The meeting's purpose, the room in which you meet, the meeting announcement, and the agenda are all examples of components of your group. What happens to one person or component affects the others. The thoughts, emotions, and physical reactions of one individual impact the thoughts, emotions, and physical reactions of others.

Consider this...... Have you ever experienced yourself feeling good and then you walk into a meeting and SUDDENLY that good feeling turns into anger or despair or confusion? Your energy has shifted. You might consider that you have walked into a "toxic pool" of energy.

Everyone experiences toxicity differently. Someone sensitive to sounds may experience toxicity as a shrilled sound or as screaming cells. Someone sensitive in the kinesthetic body may feel dirty and want a shower. Someone who has a tendency to get headaches may find that a headache is stimulated when entering an area that is energetically toxic. A stomach that tends to be weak may feel queasy when entering a toxic pool of energy.

This dynamic reaction may tempt us to blame someone else for this experience. For example, "Meetings in this company make me sick." Such responses only defer dealing directly with the problem and usually *add* to the problem. Instead of blaming, this is an ideal time to shift our own awareness to ways in which we can release the toxicity or clear the confusion. This results in a release and clearing for ourselves as well as for others.

All frustrations, tensions, emotions, and thoughts have a residue or counterpart in the energy field -- the energy field that surrounds every object, person, place, or idea. We may have a tendency to believe that yesterday's anger is gone today, but it is *not* gone from the energy field unless someone INTENTIONALLY dissolves or releases it. Unresolved issues do not disappear into healthy behavior unless the dense energetic is cleared. When the energetics are not cleared, the behavior or feeling or thought reappears in some form.

When the energy field is not cleared from yesterday's events, your reactions today -- feeling sick or angry or confused -- will simply be added to the pile of energetic waste. Chapter 8 covers some specific techniques for clearing the energy field.

The pain in groups these days is quite harmful -- harmful to individuals, to organizations as a whole, and to society. The pain must be cleared. In actuality, it *is* being cleared. Some methods of clearing pain are in themselves painful. Pain that is dissolved energetically is far less painful or not painful at all when compared to traditional methods. In fact, clearing pain and toxicity is often considered fun, exciting, and empowering.

Guidelines for Clearing Energetics

Each person in a group affects the energetics of the whole group and everyone in it. Anyone who wants to have a positive effect on the group, can do so with a few suggestions. Here are brief guidelines for shifting energetics from toxic or heavy to clear. Chapter 8 provides additional techniques.

Intention

A requirement for shifting energy from a toxic state to a clear one is to have a clear and specific intention to do so. Many techniques work when intention is clear. In fact, no technique at all is needed when intention is totally clear.

Attention

It is essential that we be able to hold our attention -- hold our attention on the energy, hold our attention on an idea, hold our attention on our intention. If our mind wanders easily or if we are distracted by our outer environment, practice is necessary. Ways of practicing include meditating (there are many approaches), listening to calming music, reading aloud, focusing on one project at a time.

Additional information on Intention and Attention are included later in this chapter, in the description of the *Marshall Model for Transforming Energy*.

Awareness

Another essential ingredient for shifting energetics is the awareness of the *condition* of energy. This can be particularly difficult in our own everyday environment. When we are so accustomed to living in a space -- toxic or clear -- we sometimes do not notice its state. We are more likely to notice its state after returning from a business trip or vacation. Even then, we soon readapt into the familiar toxicity.

Or perhaps we resolve to exit, to leave, or to resign. Leaving a situation, however, does not solve the problem or eradicate the toxicity. If we choose to leave a problem without a resolution, we will recreate a similar situation elsewhere until we learn the necessary lesson. And we leave an energetic mess behind us.

Awareness is a key to all approaches in the personal growth and group development field. Clear awareness comes from silence, from freshness, from detachment, from being able to discuss with others. To become aware of energy, step gently aside from yourself and WATCH. Move your awareness from your own reaction or emotion or opinion and WATCH from a higher perspective. This watchfulness trains you to notice your impact on the world and the world's impact on you. Another label for this is "witness." A witness observes.

If we find that we are greatly impacted by our environment, greater awareness of energy allows us to have greater mastery over our life. With greater awareness, we cease to be impacted by what is outside ourself. With greater awareness, we impact our environment. When our awareness increases along with higher intention, our impact on our environment is positive, even awesome.

Openness

Openness and receptivity are required when shifting energy. Shifting energy is not simply a matter of DOING something, it is also a matter of allowing something to occur which may be beyond our present expectation. Openness includes the concept of expectancy -- expectancy, not expectations. Being open to possibilities that are not limited by our expectations is exciting. Being open to a win-win end result that we can not figure out is empowering to all involved.

When we open, we may become vulnerable. This vulnerability can be a path to empowerment, even though at the moment we feel vulnerable we may also feel weak. The initial steps on this path of discovering and clearing energetics may be messy. A willingness to open requires a willingness to open to the unknown.

Personal Clarity

In order to clear the energy field in a group or meeting, it is essential to be clear personally. *Clear* about intention. *Clear* in communications. *Clear* about feelings. *Clear* in all aspects of relating to self and others. Our most important tool is ourself.

Perfection is not required. We all have personal issues. We are human. A process of "setting aside" the personality or ego is essential to energetic clearing work. While it is important to be attentive to our own personal development, we do not want to misuse a group for our own purposes. We must have clarity about the appropriate use of self and our relationship with the group.

Indeed, sometimes it is *not* appropriate to set aside the personal issue because the group can benefit by our honesty or vulnerability. Assisting a group in shifting energy from toxic to clear requires that the clearing take place *through* someone -- probably *you*!

Practice

Shifting energy takes practice. While some shifting can happen automatically because of a person's presence, on-going actions that are in alignment with the intention to shift energy are necessary. In other words, practice, practice, practice.

Techniques are helpful because they direct our practice. As valuable as a technique may be, a deep intention to learn about energy will be the most helpful way to guide the practice.

For example, we may decide to hold this intention: *to practice clearing energy effectively in groups.* If we remind ourself of that intention regularly, we will soon find ourself clearing energy effectively in groups. We may enroll in a workshop where someone demonstrates energetic clearing techniques, even though this was not obvious by the advance workshop information. Or, a friend may send us an article about energy clearing, even if we did not tell our friend about our intention. Our intention leads us to the information and to practice what we want to learn.

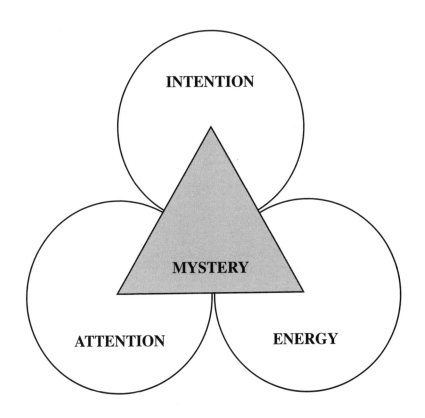

MARSHALL MODEL for TRANSFORMING ENERGY

These four key elements assist us in focusing on creative, meaningful experiences in groups, as well as other aspects of our life. The elements are connected in such a way that one cannot really be considered without the others.

INTENTION

Intention is powerful. It lays the foundation for our attitudes and actions. Sometimes we are aware of our intention, sometimes not. Intention carries a discernible vibration. Clear, high intention has a clear, high vibration. It is usually accompanied by the vibration and actions of integrity and trust and honesty.

Muddied, low intention has a muddied, low vibration. Words and actions in alignment with muddied, low vibration might be dishonesty or confusion or vindictiveness.

Actions arise from our intention. When we hold a high level of clear intention, especially when it is articulated, the methods for reaching our goals usually become obvious and our thoughts and actions become more authentic. The most effective individuals have intention that is aligned with all aspects of life that produce results that serve the highest good of all.

Several examples of high intention are: to be a non-anxious presence; for the highest good; to be an opening for peace to express itself; to create an environment that is conducive to honest communication and fair interactions.

Consider for a moment...... What is *your* intention with respect to your group? The following questions can guide you in observing intention at meetings. The more you ask questions, the higher your intention will become, even if occasionally you are displeased with an answer. Also, the intention of others around you will lift.

QUESTIONS ABOUT INTENTION

What is the intention?
What is my (your, our, their, her, his) intention?
Is this intention high enough?
What is a higher intention?
How does one intention align with another intention?
What actions are likely to follow from the intention?

ATTENTION

To create meaningful experiences, we need to hold our attention on those aspects we have identified as important. Rather than through concentration, this focusing of attention comes as a result of clarity of vision, sorting of priorities, and surrender to a higher purpose.

The key question is "*Where* is the attention?" Is the attention on the problems or the solutions? Is it on the goals or the barriers to the goals? These questions are related to the old, familiar quotation, "Is the glass half full or half empty?" *Where* is the attention?

Centering (see Chapter 7) and personal practices such as yoga, meditation, and physical exercise can assist us in holding attention as a regular part of life. Holding attention, especially in the silence, moves us to deep knowingness.

It is essential for group leaders and participants to know if and when the attention is on the proper subject. If a participant walks into the room after the meeting has started, the attention goes to the late-comer. A spilled glass of water draws attention away from the speaker. An attentive speaker recognizes this dynamic and either stops talking or repeats the ideas that were expressed at the time of the interruption.

Examples of intention about attention are: "My attention is on the purpose." And, "I hold my attention on the most important issues." And, "I focus on the items that are worthy of my attention."

Consider for a moment...... Where is *your* attention with respect to your group? The following questions can guide you in observing and holding attention at meetings, as well as other aspects of your life.

QUESTIONS ABOUT ATTENTION

Where is the attention?
Where is my (your, our, their, her, his) attention?
Is the attention on the most appropriate place?
How do I (you, we, they, she, he) determine appropriate focus?
How can the attention be shifted to where it needs to be?

ENERGY

Each item has an energy field around it that can be perceived by sensitive persons. The energy field also impacts non-sensitive persons, even though they may not be aware of it. This energy field supports, underpins, and impacts the physical level of reality.

All too often, we stay fixated in the physical, trying to "fix" what hurts there. Some believe a problem is "solved" because the annoying symptoms have dissolved or moved away. Most of this tinkering is a temporary solution because we have not gone deep enough into the energy field to make changes there. Sometimes well-meaning tinkering worsens a situation.

Energy is the life force of our experiences. Most individuals use only a portion of the energy available to them. As we become more aware of how energy surrounds and impacts us, we can release untapped resources. These untapped resources can be a path to empowerment.

When the energy is scattered, we may find it difficult to hold our attention. When the energy field is blocked, we may have difficulty remembering important information. When blocked energy produces pain, we may have difficulty being productive.

Consider for a moment...... What happens to *your* energy with respect to your group? The following questions can guide you in observing energy at meetings. Regular use of these questions can be considered a technique for gaining greater awareness of energy.

QUESTIONS ABOUT ENERGY

What is happening to the energy?
What is happening to my (your, our, their, her, his) energy?
What is worthy of our investment of personal or group energy?
What is the quality of the energy (here)?
Where is the energy blocked?
Where is the energy flowing smoothly?
How can I (you, we, they, she, he) enhance the quality of the energy?

MYSTERY

And much remains unknown. When we honor the mystery, the invisible, the uncertain, the higher power, we are more able to live in the present moment. Each present moment creates our experiences.

It is popular to say that "Spirit works in mysterious ways" or "God works in mysterious ways." True. We can expect miracles when we open to Spirit, but we cannot predict what the miracles will be. We can hope, we can pray, we can think that we are controlling Spirit, but when we acknowledge the Divine, we need to get our little egos (or perhaps big egos!) out of the way and let Spirit do the work.

At meetings, mysteries can prevail: the mysteries of Spirit as well as the mysteries of humans. Our individual personalities, skills, history, interests, and agendas show up to interact with others. The more that leaders and participants can bring the unknown into the known, the more creativity will evolve. In other words, creativity and mastery occur when mystery is brought into ordinary awareness.

Consider for a moment...... What is the mystery with respect to *your* group? The following questions can guide you in observing mystery at meetings and uplift your awareness in all parts of your life.

QUESTIONS ABOUT MYSTERY

What are the unanswered questions?
What are my (your, our, their, her, his) unanswered questions?
What are the unknowns?
Where can we go to obtain the necessary information?
What must I (you, we, they, she, he) accept as unknowable for now?
Is it time to open to an unexplored way of thinking, being, or doing?
How do we change mystery to mastery? (More is involved than changing the *y* to an *a.)*

Energy at Work

Energy works for us, with us, and as us. In the work place, a greater sensitivity to energy assists us in empowerment, effectiveness, and efficiency. Energy implies movement. When energy is blocked, we are less creative and satisfied.

Enhancing our awareness of energy will assist us *right now*. In the future, we will have an even greater need to be aware of energy to facilitate the ever-increasing acceleration of creativity and intuition. It is our responsibility to direct this flow of accelerating energy so that we focus on the areas that are worthy of our attention.

We have all noticed the increase in activity and creativity. We have more and more of everything. We have more ideas than we can carry out. We have more technology than most individuals can comprehend. With more and more, we must be more discerning than ever about how to invest our energy -- at work, at play, at home, in the world.

The next chapter focuses on deepening the understanding of the needs and dynamics of groups. Our sensitivity to these needs and dynamics assists us in creating energetic meetings that are empowering and satisfying.

Chapter 4

Group
Needs
and
Dynamics

Harmony at Meetings

Disharmony or conflict at meetings is inevitable. While a reasonable amount of conflict can be creative and enriching, conflict that is not properly managed can be harmful. Interpersonal conflicts -- as contrasted to conflicts of ideas or principles -- are in special need of careful management. Seeing conflict or disharmony as the expression of differences helps to take the fear from conflict.

Living in conscious harmony is like playing in a symphony -- and knowing that we are playing in a symphony. At any given moment our section of the symphony may be in temporary harmony or temporary disharmony. Both group members and instrumentalists must have the conscious intention to strive for harmony without being discouraged by the momentary note of disharmony that adds interest to the experience.

The symphony's composer wrote a score which the conductor interprets and the musicians play with different instruments, in their own style, according to their ability. At some times, we are more aware of one instrument than another. Or we hear a solo or a duet.

When we listen deeply to the music, we notice space between the notes: rhythm. Colors and tones and volume add texture and interest: timbre. We have different responses to different parts: feelings.

Satisfaction increases when everyone in the orchestra reads at the same place on the same sheet of music. At some times it is important for a musician to play softly to blend with the rest of the sounds. Other times, it is important to play loudly, even being the center of attention. Rhythms may change, even in the middle of a piece. Sounds may "fight" with each other to heighten drama before leading to resolution.

Joy happens when everyone perceives the symphony as all One, with each instrument playing an important part. In order to live in conscious harmony, we must embrace the concept that we are all One.

Procedures that Promote Group Satisfaction

Groups can avoid or reduce the likelihood of difficulties at meetings by adopting certain procedures as standard. Here are some key procedures.

Clarify Purpose. A group's clear purpose right from its beginning helps all other considerations and actions to become clearer.

Establish Climate for Sharing. Whenever possible, arrange for participant comfort. Here are suggestions:
- Provide name tags;
- Place chairs for all to see each other;
- Allow everyone the opportunity to speak;
- Protect the rights of individuals to have dissenting opinions and to change their opinions.

Explain Ground Rules. Let group members know what is expected; check their understanding and acceptance of procedures. Ask if they have questions about certain ground rules or give them choices that help them to interpret the ground rules. If the group is new, be certain that the members are involved in establishing the ground rules.

Set Goal(s). Develop meeting goals with the group and refer to them often as the meeting progresses. As goals are reached, be certain that specific individuals and the group as a whole are acknowledged and applauded.

Reveal Agenda. Announce items to be covered and the meeting's structure and process. Written agendas emphasize meeting focus and hold participants' attention. When practical, allow group members to participate in agenda setting. Agendas distributed in advance allow participants to think through important items so the meeting is more productive and meaningful.

Be Task-oriented. Focus on the task and not on personalities or irrelevant issues. Be careful, though, not to be so task-oriented that the group overlooks or shortchanges interpersonal relationships.

Listen to Everyone. Acknowledge group members and their ideas. Not all ideas must be pursued, used, or evaluated, but all need to be received. Leaders and participants take the first step in showing that they are listening by giving direct eye contact to the speaker. Calling participants by name and referring to the comments they have made are indications that group members are listening and hearing each other.

Monitor the Energy. If the vitality of the group wanes, notice and take actions to work with lowered energy. Sometimes it is appropriate to slow down, suggest silence, or take a break. Other times, it is appropriate to take an action that uplifts the energy. Other chapters in this book assist you in monitoring and shifting energy.

Reflect Together on the Process and Task. Periodically, talk with each other about perceptions of a meeting or a series of meetings. Ask participants if they are satisfied or want to suggest changes. You might from time to time suggest changes to test a group's willingness to look at itself. Without a specific time devoted to reflection, groups -- both participants and leaders -- can make assumptions about satisfaction of others. Reflection with others increases choices for improvement.

Embrace an Intention of Empowerment. Decide that every meeting is an opportunity for everyone to be empowered. You can meet the opportunity with vitality and inspiration.

As we conduct and attend meetings, we need to use good sense. Each group, each meeting is unique. Experiment to find the techniques and style that produce the most productive results for each meeting.

Group Development

The field of group dynamics is blessed with many windows for looking at the developmental stages of groups. If you are interested in this area, you will want to follow up with books or learning events that focus specifically on group development.

Once we have adopted a window for looking at groups that makes sense to us, we see groups in a new way. For example, we are more likely to be able to assist groups through their developmental phases rather than fearing the groups or their phases. We replace annoyance with compassion; resistance with acceptance.

Novice leaders, trainers, and consultants often think they have done something "wrong" when a group acts in a particular way. By understanding group dynamics, we are less likely to blame ourselves or anyone else when the group becomes uncomfortable. Instead, we assist the group through a challenging time.

A helpful and memorable method for perceiving the stages of a group was developed by B.W. Tuckman. This model -- or window -- for looking at groups can be helpful to everyone involved in a group in any way. Following the discussion of these stages, a new paradigm for group development is presented. It is a simple window, but one that may have more meaning after exploring a more traditional model.

Here are the stages: forming, storming, norming, and performing. Others have added "transforming." This model is applicable to the overall life of a group. The model can also be used to see the dynamics of a single meeting of a group which meets regularly.

As with all developmental and other human relationship models, this describes a process. Although the stages of group development are presented in a step-by-step way, they are not linear, Keep in mind that aspects of the group can be in different stages at a given time. An incident can shift the group from one stage to another quickly, especially if not well established in a stage. Key components of these five stages follow.

Forming Stage

The forming stage begins when the group is first conceived and continues until its formation is complete. Technically, the group is *not* a group, but either an idea of a subgroup of one or more individuals or a collection of individuals. Meaningful and well-managed experiences in this stage are particularly helpful during the next stage.

Participant Questions. The expressed or thought questions are: *Why am I here? Who else is here? Why are they here? Do I belong in this group? How do I compare to others in the group?*

Characteristic Behavior and Feelings. The most characteristic behavior patterns are politeness and confusion. Most individuals are eager to give a good first impression. Confusion may arise about simple things like location of rest rooms, best sitting place, names, other unknowns.

Participant Issues. The primary individual issue can be best captured by the word "safety." Participants want to know if they will be safe and they want to know what they need to do to make or keep themselves safe. Safety refers to physical, emotional, mental, and spiritual needs.

Group Issues. In the forming stage, the primary group issue revolves around the criteria for membership. Status in the organization, educational background, longevity in a job, age, gender, race, are a few examples of criteria. Issues around diversity and homogeneity are important at this stage. If persons attend inappropriately, the group may not get beyond the forming stage. Confusion will surround the group or force it to re-form or reform.

Energetic Considerations. In the forming stage, the energy field is seeking its distinction. The energy is likely to be static or confused or shallow. If the group gathers in a place that has a clean energy field, it has a better chance of clarifying direction and connecting with its mission.

Leadership Issues. The participants are dependent on the leader or the person calling the meeting. They tend to look for direction to start the meeting and to guide it in a meaningful way. It is commonplace for participants to look to *anyone* who appears to be in the know.

Storming Stage

The group is in the storming stage when participants act out, sometimes like teenagers. Good humor, appreciation, and acceptance are keys to moving through this stage into the next.

Participant Questions. The questions in participants' minds or on their lips are: *Who is in charge? Where are we going? What is happening? What if we do not do what we are supposed to do? What do I have to do or say to get my needs met?*

Characteristic Behavior and Feelings. Differences that were exposed in the forming stage are now challenged. Assumed differences or similarities may also be challenged. Feelings of confusion can deepen into argument. Acting out concerns about power or control is common. We might generally characterize the behavior as "immature" or "pushy."

Participant Issues. This is a time of establishing power and individuality. Healthy movement through this stage is facilitated by a high degree of tolerance for individual differences and even encouragement to express those differences.

Group Issues. The group is pushing to create an acceptable process for decision-making and problem-solving. Processes for allowing issues to come out in the open are helpful now, especially if such processes were not used during the forming stage. Moving too quickly to agreement to avoid discomfort is generally unwise.

Energetic Considerations. Feelings are often tense in this storming stage. The energy tends to move in a counterclockwise direction, which is uncomfortable, especially to sensitive persons.

Leadership Issues. The group tends to be counterdependent. That is, one or more persons are likely to attack or criticize the official leader or others in visible roles. The counterdependent behavior may be very subtle. Novice leaders often take this behavior personally. Experienced and effective leaders simply allow the behavior to happen with appropriate response (including silence), without attacking back or taking actions personally.

Norming Stage

Norms and patterns develop in the norming stage. That is, the group knows that it is establishing itself as a group with its own history and procedures and rituals.

Participant Questions. Participants are most likely to be asking or thinking such questions as: *How can we come to a decision on this? What will assist us as a group? What do we want to do about that? How do you (I, we, he, she, they) feel about that?*

Characteristic Behavior and Feelings. Behavior patterns include sharing information and processes that facilitate the success of the group. Someone in the group is able to make generalizations about how the group is functioning, and possibly also how *well* the group is functioning. Norms imposed or suggested earlier by authority are freely examined.

Participant Issues. This stage is measured by and fosters meaningful relationships among participants. Collaboration rather than competition is beginning to find expression. As identity with the group strengthens, individual power issues are at a minimum or nonexistent if the group is to remain in this stage or move to the next.

Group Issues. The group negotiates openly about roles, tasks, time, and agendas. Differences are embraced at a level that allows listening to deepen. Routine -- and perhaps boredom -- can set in if the group becomes complacent or adamant about its norms.

Energetic Considerations. A group that is firmly in the norming stage can be lively or quiet, as appropriate. The energetic bonds between pairs of individuals are obvious to those who can perceive the energy field. Participants are content to let each person have his or her own turn as the focus of attention.

Leadership Issues. Interdependency characterizes the leadership. An official leader may or may not be active. Anyone in the group can offer leadership qualities and skills. When participants do not want these offerings, negotiation occurs if the group is to remain in the norming stage, otherwise, the group can revert to storming or (re)forming.

Performing Stage

The group is in the performing stage when participants are balanced in their attention on people and task. The group attends to the needs of participants while it performs its task. This is a "team" in the deepest sense of today's meaning of the term. The group has its own personality.

Participant Questions. Silent and verbalized questions include: *What more can I do to support this group? Does everyone understand what is happening? Is there any more that we must do or say (today or before...... or by next meeting, etc.)?*

Characteristic Behavior and Feelings. Participants have a sense of "groupness." They care about each other *and* the task. The patterns and norms established in the previous stage are embraced by all.

Participant Issues. Individuals know each other. They also tend to trust each other or at least know the areas in which to trust each other. If trust is broken, the group moves out of this stage into one of the previous stages. Control issues are minimal or nonexistent.

Group Issues. The group knows its task and accomplishes it. The intelligence of the group knows on whom to depend and allows for shifting of responsibilities as needed.

Energetic Considerations. The energy field is balanced and smooth. The passing of information and resources throughout the group is even and clear. When there is an interruption in the smooth flow, the group energy field is impacted. Minor interruptions can easily be mended by the healthy state of an established intention and mission; major interruptions must be attended to by the whole group or the group reverts to an earlier stage.

Leadership Issues. Leadership functions are characterized by interdependency. While an official leader may be active, this person works with others in a way that fosters the good of the whole.

Transforming Stage

This stage is relevant for only certain groups. A group is in the transforming stage when it terminates and reconvenes or when its mission is redefined. Here are two examples: (1) participants in a training event want a reunion, and (2) a task force creates an on-going group with related or unrelated purpose.

Participant Questions. Expressed or thought questions are: *How can we keep in touch? Shall we come together again? How will this new experience (task, content, participants, feelings, etc.) be different from or the same as the current or last one?* And, to some extent, variations on the questions listed in the Forming Stage above are relevant here.

Characteristic Behavior and Feelings. Underlying issues of how and if to terminate or re-group show themselves in a variety of feelings and behavior patterns. Grief and abandonment issues are common.

Participant Issues. The primary participant issues are based in the fact that participants have had shared experiences. Whether unnamed or named "good," "bad," or "indifferent," the experiences are, nonetheless, shared. Loyalty and confidentiality issues may be explored or redefined.

Group Issues. The group issues revolve around separation and remaining together, feelings which may be mixed throughout the group and within individual participants.

Energetic Considerations. Individuals who have had shared experiences also have ties to each other. These ties or "bonds of connection" are visible to anyone who is trained to see the energy field. Negative bonds -- which can be cut without interfering with positive bonds -- need to be severed so that participants can work in other groups without being drained by bonding to this group.

Leadership Issues. In this stage, typically the group takes over leadership, even if one person remains the official leader. When the group has progressed through the following stages fully, tugs for position are rare. The introduction of a new leader -- especially a manager -- may push a group into the transforming stage and/or back to the (re)forming.

Applying the Stages to a Group which Meets Successively

Forming. Each time a group comes together, it goes through developmental stages. Even though we may consider that a group has generally reached the "norming stage," when it reconvenes, it must re-form and sometimes storm before it reconnects with the patterns and norms. A wise leader allows time at each meeting for appropriate "forming" strategies through such activities as introductions or refreshments or networking or asking for brief updates since the last meeting.

Storming. Groups which are constantly attentive to honoring diversity may not need to explore the storming stage repeatedly. Wise leaders, however, do not make assumptions that even the most effective "performing" groups will never storm again. When the group or anyone in it acts in unpredictable ways, storming can occur or perhaps has occurred. At times, storming may need to be encouraged.

Norming and **Performing.** A group that operated at the last meeting in the norming or performing stage, may not be ready to operate at that level in the current meeting. Here are a few variables that can interfere with a group's immediate return to the norming or performing stage: a new participant, a redefined task, afterthoughts from any participant, an absent member.

Clearly, any rigid application of these stages of group development will be unrealistic, perhaps even frustrating. Consider this model a window through which to explore the life of groups. Clean or open the window when necessary. And, by all means, break it when it no longer serves you.

New Paradigm for Group Development

Through a window I will call the "New Paradigm," we see groups from a new perspective, an energetic perspective. It stretches those who must see everything in the concrete. If you are stretched or are not willing to look, simply pass by this small section. It will wait for another time.

Every group has a mission which can be seen in the energy field as a sphere. It is up to the participants of the group to *open* to this mission in order to receive it. This requires letting go of the ego that believes that we "create" the mission. Such letting go can be difficult for leaders who have been considered successful because they have "made things happen."

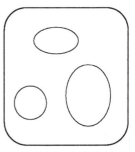

Spheres*

In the New Paradigm, we *allow* life to happen, with a maximum of joy and a minimum of control and struggle. *We receive* instead of take. *We collaborate* instead of compete. *We believe in abundance* rather than lack. *We seek ways to empower ourselves and facilitate others' empowerment* instead of trying to take control. *We put more faith in the invisible* than in the visible. *We know that we are interconnected. We trust our intuition.*

And what we know is true for ourselves we also know is true for others. That is, we know that others have feelings and intuitive insights. We know that others are interconnected with the same whole.

In the New Paradigm, the direction for seeking solutions is inward rather than outward. As the attention changes to a more balanced focus of the inner creating the outer, transformation accelerates.

A group that spends time in silence together more easily discovers its mission and the solutions to its problems. This takes practice, of course. Recognized techniques that are now used to enhance group effectiveness are still useful, but find their place as *part* of the experience rather than the reason for change.

A group that honors Spirit is guided into the New Paradigm. You may call Spirit by other names, such as The Divine, Creator, Higher Power, The One, the Universe, God, Higher Self, higher consciousness. The New Paradigm is not new at all. It is the original intention of life: Peace on Earth, living in loving support to and from one another.

* Taken from the *Symbolic Language of Energy*, By Jeanie Marshall

Considerations for Groups

Here are some considerations for anyone starting, leading, or participating in a group. Each group will have its own set of needs and unique relationship to these considerations.

Purpose or Mission. A clearly articulated group purpose greatly enhances a group's experience. Ideally, the group participants themselves formulate the purpose statement. As new members are invited to participate in an established group, the written purpose statement can be used as an introduction.

Commitment. It is essential that the leader and each member understand and be committed to the purpose and the decisions of the group. A leader may want to state his or her own commitment and ask the members to consider and articulate theirs.

Responsibility. Leaders and group members have distinct responsibilities which they need to understand and embrace. Clear responsibilities are more likely to yield clear actions.

Diversity. Individuals are different. Their differences need to be exposed, recognized, affirmed, and integrated into discussions and decisions. If all group members have the same opinions, no need exists for a group. It is, however, generally helpful for members of the group to have the same basic understanding of the group's purpose and similar deeply held values.

Accountability. Individual members and the group as a whole are accountable for the actions of the group, unless it is clear that someone else is accountable. Accountability not only enhances responsibility, it also enhances satisfaction and dedication.

Energy. An energy field is established whenever a group is established. That energy field grows as the group expands its membership, tasks, and outreach. All decisions and outputs are coded in the energy field, as are dynamics such as integrity, fairness, harmony. A group may meet in a location in which the energy field has energetics and information that is related to persons and issues outside the group.

Quality. Decisions can enhance or maintain quality in a group's product or service. Examining process and searching for more effective ways to work enhance quality of the group's life.

Size. The size of the group depends on its purpose. Groups that are too small may not represent others well nor include enough diversity; groups that are too large may have difficulty making decisions.

Attendance. Groups that have a norm of full attendance tend to operate the most efficiently. When absence is unavoidable, consider adopting the norm that members inform the appropriate person that they cannot attend. Consider also acknowledging absent members at the meeting and updating them afterward.

Membership. Clear rules and rights of membership establish boundaries and expectations. Ordinarily a group has a fixed or specific membership; that is, the names of the members are known. Groups can also have loose or unrestricted membership allowing for participants to attend who are not known to others.

Late-comers. Persons who arrive late to meetings present challenges for the leaders, other meeting participants, and the late-comers themselves. Finding a balance between updating the late-comer and honoring those who have arrived on time is important. A facilitator can often acknowledge late-comers with a few words without disturbing the flow of business.

Facilitator/Leader. One or more persons convene the group and attend to leadership functions. Group members need to understand the functions of the leadership role. This role and the corresponding functions may rotate. While effective leaderless groups do exist, they are rare, and, when they do exist, ordinarily are small and develop from the foundation of an effectively led group.

Decisions. Over time, an effective group will use various methods of decision-making. The ideal method most of the time is consensus, which means that everyone accepts the decision that is reached. Consensus does not mean "agreement," but acceptance. See Chapter 7 for additional information on decision-making methods.

As Groups Change, Needs Change

Every group has unique needs, just as each individual does. Some of these needs we can generalize about and develop models to explain. As groups continue to mature and move out of the old, outdated ways of being, the needs and dynamics will change.

We know that we are in the New Meeting Paradigm when individuals easily collaborate, willingly share information, and are excited about participating at meetings. We know that we are in the New Meeting Paradigm when participants support and encourage effective leaders. We know that we are in the New Meeting Paradigm when everyone leaves meetings feeling energized and empowered.

The next chapter focuses on ideas to enhance your meetings by making effective arrangements. Your advance preparation and consideration can be pivotal in successful, energetic meetings. Your follow-through after meetings is just as significant as the preparations and the meetings themselves.

Chapter 5

Meeting Arrangements

Arranging the Meeting Place

Perhaps the details of your meeting are already established. If so, you may want to review these pages for future reference or to improve your current meeting accommodations or format.

If you need to arrange a meeting place, you will want to pay attention to the following items that pertain to your group's needs. If someone else is arranging the meeting, you can use these items to assist others or remind them of details that help create a climate of positive energy.

You may also find this chapter helpful if you want to construct a questionnaire for your meeting participants or planners to determine the elements that are the most crucial to the success of your meeting.

Selecting the Place

To select the appropriate place for your group, it will help if you have clear questions in mind. Asking the questions during the selection period will reduce frustrations on the day of the meeting.

Location. *Is the location accessible to those who are expected to attend?* Attendance tends to improve if finding the place and getting there are convenient.

Room(s). *Is one large room needed or are several small ones better for your meeting? Will the room comfortably hold the number of persons expected?* Moveable chairs are preferable to auditorium seating when you want audience participation and essential when you want participants to interact with each other.

Size. *Is the room big enough? Or too big? If small discussion groups are planned, can the groups be separated so one group neither influences nor annoys another?* A carpeted floor helps to minimize noise when a large group divides into small groups in the same room.

Accessibility for the Physically Challenged. *Is the building accessible?* Society has become increasingly aware of the responsibility to make facilities accessible to all. Legal requirements demand accessibility, but some meeting rooms or rest rooms may be inadequate. Check them out, even if you do not expect a participant with a wheelchair.

Environment. *Is the location cheerful or depressing? Is the lighting adequate? If depressing or dark, what can be done to make the space bright and inviting?* Chair arrangements, auxiliary lighting, plants, or posters can change the atmosphere of a room.

Appropriate Space. *Is the room conducive to conducting the meeting as you have planned it? For example, can you hang flip charts on the wall or use an overhead projector, if needed? Can chairs be moved for small groupings? Are tables needed for display or writing?* Ingenuity can do wonders for a room that may at first seem imperfect.

Climate Control. *Can you control the heating and cooling? Do you have access to fresh air? Does the facility have smoking rules? If not, do you need to make some for the group?* Advance consideration adds to the comfort of all.

Other Advance Questions and Considerations

Directions. *Are written directions available for travelers? Is parking adequate?* Try to make it as convenient as possible, especially for those who are attending for the first time.

Refreshments. *Do you want to serve food and drinks? Are there restrictions about refreshments? Are equipment and supplies provided or must you supply them?* Check all aspects in advance to avoid uncomfortable surprises. Delegate hospitality tasks to a dependable individual or individuals who enjoy playing host or hostess.

Equipment and Supplies. *What are your needs and who will supply them?* Equipment may include flip chart stands, chalk boards, tables and chairs, overhead projector and screen. Supplies may include flip chart paper, markers, masking tape, chalk, and program materials.

Advance Information for Participants

Publicity. Getting the right persons at the meeting is crucial to its success. The meeting purpose needs to be stated clearly to draw the appropriate persons who understand and share the goals.

Pre-registration. If your meeting requires registration, a precise deadline facilitates more efficient planning for presenters, materials, room assignments, parking, and refreshments. State clearly if pre-registration is required, preferred, or unnecessary.

Participant Preparation. Consider what else participants may need to be informed about: time, resources to research or bring, clothing to wear, telephone numbers for emergency, etc.

The Meeting Day: Personal Considerations

Name Tags. While some individuals resist wearing name tags, most appreciate seeing others' names. When participants make their own name tags, provide wide-tipped markers and writing area. When name tags are prepared in advance, be certain names are spelled correctly and supply a few blank tags for corrections or unexpected participants.

To facilitate reading name tags at a distance, legible printing with a black marker or a large readable font on a computer works best. A ball point pen or small typewriter print helps only those within a foot or two of the person wearing the name tag.

Leader/Presenter Availability. Leaders who greet and meet participants in advance of the meeting tend to be more comfortable when the session begins. Participants usually appreciate this gesture and may even lose confidence if leaders scurry around to finish last minute details, review notes, or arrive late. If you have invited an outside leader or facilitator, be certain she or he has all the details about time and place and other expectations.

Greeters. If your meeting is large or if guests or newcomers are expected, official greeters add friendliness to your gathering.

The Meeting Day: Physical Considerations

Confidence, not Complacency. Have confidence and trust in those you have contracted for service and do not take anything for granted. Arrive early to assure yourself that your needs are addressed.

Directions to Site. Post signs, if necessary, to give adequate directions to the building and/or rooms. If participants move from room to room for different sessions, adequate signs speed the movement.

Set-up. The room arranged twenty minutes before registration begins leaves leaders free to greet participants and be available for questions. Identify tasks for early participants who offer to help.

Registration Table. The registrar will probably be the first person the participants meet. Consequently, this person needs to be friendly, inviting, and knowledgeable about the registration process. Even when no fees are collected, a registration table is important if you are to collect names and addresses of participants.

Resources Table. If you or others attending the meeting have materials to show, a separate table is helpful. This allows participants to browse among the materials before or after the meeting and during breaks. If you want participants to display their resources, be certain to let them know in advance.

Musical Background. Appropriate background music can add to setting the desired mood before the meeting and during breaks.

Checklist for Effective Meetings

This checklist is designed for use by all meeting participants, especially the leader and/or facilitator. Some items may be more or less relevant for each meeting experience.

Prior to the Meeting

____ 1.   Identify the (my, our) intention for the group:

_____

____ 2.   Decide if anyone needs to be invited to attend (regular participants and guests).

_____

____ 3.   Invite appropriate persons, giving them all the relevant data to prepare and to arrive on time.

____ 4.   Plan the meeting:

    ____ Identify facilitator or leader _____

    ____ Identify recorder or secretary _____

    ____ Set agenda; estimate time needed for each item.

    ____ Consult with or coach participants about their reports or other contributions

    ____ Other_____

____ 5.   Arrange for necessary equipment and materials.

_____

____ 6.   Arrive at the meeting room early enough to set up the physical environment and to clear the energy field. (See Chapter 8.)

____ 7.   Center yourself. (See Chapter 7.)

____ 8.   Consider what else needs to be done to ensure a successful meeting of empowered participants.

At the Beginning of the Meeting

_____ 9.   Start on time.

_____ 10.   Remind yourself of high intention (e.g., *the highest good of all concerned*).

_____ 11.   Arrange seating so everyone can see everyone, if possible.

_____ 12.   Model strong listening skills from the outset of the meeting.

_____ 13.   State or develop ground rules or other expectations for the meeting; define roles.

_____ 14.   Present agenda and negotiate changes. Or, develop the agenda with the group.

_____ 15.   Review action steps from previous meetings or other history that brings the whole group up to date.

_____ 16.   Introduce guests or new members; acknowledge absent members.

_____ 17.   Notice if participants seem centered; if not, introduce centering concept or activity. (See Chapter 7.)

During the Meeting

_____ 18.   Continue to remind yourself of your high intention (e.g., *to foster open communications; that everyone feels empowered by this meeting*).

_____ 19.   Spend adequate time defining the problem prior to working on solutions.

_____ 20.   Listen to participants' comments for evidence of hidden agendas or misunderstandings or other behavior that may be difficult. (See Chapter 9.)

_____ 21.   Send congruent messages; be consistent.

_____ 22. Confront dysfunctional behavior without offending group members. See Chapter 10 for specific suggestions on difficult behavior.

_____ 23. Summarize points made by the group or ask someone else to summarize.

_____ 24. Attend to both process and content, integrating the two.

_____ 25. Keep checking the energy. Is it light or dense? Is it comfortable or uncomfortable? Is it high or low? Your sensitivity increases as you use the techniques in this book.

_____ 26. Envision the energy moving in a clockwise direction around the group or around the room.

_____ 27. Maintain a list of the ideas that are generated, passing ideas to appropriate persons inside or outside the group.

_____ 28. Pace the meeting. As appropriate, keep the group moving and on schedule or slow down or stop.

_____ 29. Determine appropriate time for making decisions and clarifying action steps.

_____ 30. Make group decisions by the most appropriate method. Whenever possible, decide by consensus. (See Chapter 7.)

At the End of the Meeting

_____ 31. Summarize and make action steps explicit.

_____ 32. Confirm next meeting date and set preliminary agenda.

_____ 33. Reflect on the meeting as a group. Ascertain that the actions taken are in alignment with the group's mission, purpose, or intent.

_____ 34.   Close meeting positively and decisively, on time. If the meeting needs to run beyond the announced time, check with the participants to be certain that is acceptable. Meetings that end with participants drifting out are usually quite unsatisfactory.

_____ 35.   Ask the group if everyone is leaving the group feeling empowered. (If you do not ask the group this question, at least ask yourself if you believe everyone leaves feeling empowered.)

_____ 36.   Clean up energetic messes that the meeting may have created physically, emotionally, mentally, or spiritually. An energy clearing will leave the room lighter for the next group. (See Chapter 8.)

After the Meeting

_____ 37.   Distribute meeting minutes or other reports that emphasize action steps and empowering ideas.

_____ 38.   Check to see what else needs to be done to have closure on the meeting.

_____ 39.   Contact group members to see if they need help to meet their commitments or to gain greater clarity.

_____ 40.   Plan for the next meeting.

And Now the Climate is Set

The information in this section has been designed to assist you in understanding groups and energy so that your meetings will be conducive to generating contributions that accomplish your goals. In the next section, we focus on generating those positive contributions while the group participants are at meetings.

Generating Positive Contributions

Leaders, group facilitators, and others who are responsible for the success of meetings generally want to encourage positive results from positive individuals. Unfortunately, few models exist of truly empowered groups or meetings.

Empowered persons actively participating at meetings are most likely to achieve the goals set at meetings. Empowered persons tend to empower others and keep themselves empowered by monitoring inner thoughts and feelings. Empowerment is an inner dynamic which is demonstrated by our outer actions and words.

Certain strategies and techniques can uplift individual participation and model constructive sharing of information, ideas, and opinions. Some form of evaluation following a meeting makes us attentive to the areas which call for change or applause.

Chapter 6

Empowered
Persons
at
Meetings

Who is Empowered?

If *you* are empowered, *I* am empowered.
If you are *disempowered,* I am *not* empowered.

Empowerment comes from a power *inside,* not *outside.*
When guided by high intention
this power is used for the good of all.

Competition leads us to believe that resources are limited.
When we turn within, we recognize that
creativity is unlimited, leading us to unlimited resources.

We are empowered by unlimited power.
We compete when we believe that power is limited.

Today, help someone else to be empowered.
Such an act will empower you.

Empowerment at Meetings

Empowered persons empower and energize meetings. Disempowered persons disempower and de-energize meetings. Energy around and emitted from someone who is empowered is different from that of a person who is disempowered. The energy of two empowered persons will be somewhat similar, and perhaps more similar than their actions.

What does it really mean to be "empowered"? It means an individual has accessed resources within himself or herself and is confident of being able to be or do something. Empowered managers are those who know they can manage the people and tasks and do so, ideally through empowered employees. Empowered meeting participants allow ideas to flow through them and express them in meetings.

Empowered persons are balanced, confident, vital, and ready. The word itself has potency and strength. Those who are empowered are not depressed, confused, or wishy washy. Of course, even empowered persons have days or moments of confusion or frustration or doubt, but the predominant expression is one of confidence and strength.

To acquaint ourselves with the energetics of empowerment, we find it helpful to watch persons whom we consider to be empowered. As we observe, we collect data about energy that we experience around, from, and in these persons. We can notice how others are impacted by this energy.

Ordinarily, we like to be in the presence of those who are truly empowered because this energy is contagious and healing. The behavior of empowered persons is often imitated, but empowerment is not just a set of actions. Actions aligned with inner knowingness and strength are necessary for empowerment to be genuine.

Let us be clear, empowered persons do *not* get their power from other persons. Empowered persons do not hit or overpower or trample on others' rights or dominate meetings or suppress others. Since empowered persons are powered from the *inside,* they carry their power with them.

The energetics of empowerment can be described as light and free, but not "airy-fairy." Empowered energetics vibrate at a high rate. Note the common expression, "She/he has good vibes." Once we are sensitive to this vibration, we can discern immediately the state of a person's empowerment or self esteem or confidence. This discernment saves time in selecting members for a group or in appointing group participants to certain tasks.

The greater our ability is to discern the energy of empowerment, the greater is our own vitality. Discernment empowers the one who discerns.

When beginning to observe the energetics of empowerment, we focus first on behavior and other things that are audible or visible or touchable. Such qualities are in the physical dimension -- an important dimension, but not the only one. The deeper dimensions underpin and create the physical, not the other way around. So when we want a deeper understanding of what we see, hear, and touch, we need to relate to the underlying energetics.

We relate to the underlying energetics by turning within, by listening to the inner voice. Regular meditation is extremely helpful -- meditators are likely to say "essential" -- to the inner process. As we become more sensitive to dynamics that are invisible to the physical eye, we can more easily resonate to the energy of empowerment.

To be empowered, we must release outdated beliefs, dense vibrations, repressed fears and other feelings. It becomes easier to open to lighter vibrations when we have cleared ourself of density.

To be empowered, we must review our beliefs and replace those that are disempowering with those that are empowering. Our society holds many beliefs about aging, health, money, jobs, and relationships that are disempowering and false.

To be empowered, we must be conscious of our thoughts and feelings and beliefs. As we all become more sensitive to the nonphysical world, it will be increasingly more difficult to hide true feelings.

Asking Empowering Questions

We constantly ask ourselves questions. Many are silent or unconscious and often disempowering. With a shift in consciousness, these messages can be transformed; and more importantly, the impact of these messages can be transformed.

Generally, it is wise to avoid "why?" questions as they often yield blaming responses. Of course, "why?" questions that genuinely and enthusiastically probe can be empowering. Instead, we can ask how, what, when, where, etc.

When your group is in a mess, ask without any thought of blame......

What can we learn from this?
How have we benefitted from this so far?
What are the conditions that allowed this situation?

......and then......

Are we ready to have a different experience?
What do we want to bring into our reality?
What can we do now to change this situation?
How can we support each other?

Here are questions to ask yourself to enhance your personal effectiveness, which in turn, enhances your effectiveness in groups:

What excites me about today?
How can I share my gifts or talents or skills now?
What can I learn here?
What can I give today?
What am I grateful for?
How can I bring deeper meaning to this situation?
What is worthy of my attention and energy?
What brings me joy in this experience?
How can I leave this place more beautiful than I found it?
Is there someone I can help today?
How can I make a positive difference?
Who am I?

Active Participation at Meetings

Active participation at meetings leads to synergy, creativity, enhanced commitment, and empowerment. This participation, of course, needs to be managed effectively. It takes more skill to manage a meeting when participants are active than when they are passive. As with all choices, there are tradeoffs.

WARNING: If we do not want involvement from meeting participants, we need to be clear about that desire from the beginning. It is unfair and incongruent to encourage participation and then thwart it. Disempowerment results. No one wins.

Here are techniques the facilitator or leader can use to encourage participation. Participants can also suggest approaches. The meeting length, format, and regularity help to determine the appropriate techniques.

Arrange Meeting Room for Interaction. Round tables take the emphasis off the leader and promote participant interaction. Tables set up to form a square or chairs set in a circle establish equality among participants and leader, promoting group discussion. U shapes, too, promote interaction, but establish the leader as authority.

Allow Time for Participants to Get Acquainted. When participants have the opportunity to know about the others with whom they are expected to work, the process is enhanced. All are able to make more meaningful connections with people and ideas. Building a climate of trust encourages meaningful responses now and later.

Ask Questions that can be Answered by a Show of Hands. Questions need not be mutually exclusive, but ideally allow for everyone to respond at least once in a series (e.g., "How many of you are from the Arlington Plant? the Syracuse Plant? the San Francisco Plant? someplace else?). When asked early in the session, such questions allow participants a chance to get to know each other in addition to their opportunity to be actively engaged.

Listen. Show you are interested in what every participant says. Your body language, your facial expressions, and the words you say in response to each member reveal the extent to which you are listening. The leader who models the ability to listen especially at the beginning of the meeting encourages ongoing participation. Over-participation is usually minimized because individuals know that they have been heard and will be heard when making an important comment.

Elicit a Response from Everyone. Early in the meeting, ask each participant to respond to a question or comment. It may be a "getting acquainted" question (e.g., "What is the most important item on the agenda for you?") or related to the specific content area (e.g., "How do you expect your subordinates will react to this new procedure?").

Use Buzz Groups. When asking a provocative question or raising a controversial issue, divide the total group into groups of about 3-5 participants. While everyone cannot personally hear from everyone else, each will have the chance to speak to others. When the total group reconvenes, the responses will represent greater quality and depth. (See additional information about buzz groups in Chapter 7.)

Distribute Materials or Handouts. Make papers relevant to your report available prior to speaking so that participants can record their own notes. Writing is a form of involvement. It is not a favor to participants when speakers announce, "You don't need to take notes; I'll give you handouts on everything later."

Provide an Assessment or Survey. Generally, if such an assessment is used, it should not be long or complex. If it is simple enough so all participants can complete it, they will be involved and learn something about themselves. Ideally, the leader and others also learn about the group members.

Notice the Energy. A group that is passive has a small energy field. As they keep their thoughts and ideas to themselves, they also tend to withhold their energy and vitality. An actively involved group of participants has a large and lively energy field. If there is *too* much participation or if the participation is frenetic, the energy field can be scattered or fractured.

Count to Ten. When posing a question to the group, count to ten before asking a second question, restating the question, answering the question, or moving on. When speedy responses are constantly demanded, some participants may feel inadequate or discouraged about participating. By allowing more time, you show that you value all types of involvement -- silent and thoughtful as well as vocal and immediate. In addition, the quality of responses is likely to improve as the deeper ideas are added to the more obvious, quick ones on the surface.

Allow Thinking Time. When stating a problem or asking a question, ask the participants to jot down a few notes before anyone responds verbally. Since some individuals need more time than others to process information, "thinking time" allows an opportunity for these individuals to contemplate, even if they do not actually speak. It also allows deeper thinking for everyone, which leads to less obvious responses and richer discussion.

Ask What, Not If. The question "Any questions?" has become a rather automatic and sometimes rhetorical inquiry by many leaders and facilitators. Allowing a count to ten as explained above makes this question more sincere. Better yet, ask "What questions do you have?" Or, still better, state "Please take a few moments to reflect on what I've just said and consider what questions or comments you have."

Use a Variety of Activities and Approaches. Vary meeting techniques to increase overall participation. When the group stays too long in one particular mode or activity, participants lose enthusiasm and tend not to participate.

Hold an Intention for Everyone's Participation. Identify a statement or idea that supports the empowered participation of everyone. As individuals participate, you might ask yourself, *What would be the most empowering response to her comment?* Or, *What can I do that would activate his power from the inside? What would empower everyone?* Generally, empowered persons participate in ways that facilitate the forward movement of the group; disempowered persons do not. Discovering ways to assist persons out of their disempowerment can, however, empower and facilitate a whole group.

Empowerment at Work

Empowerment works for us, with us, and in us. At the work place, empowerment needs to go hand in hand with effectiveness and efficiency. Since we are all interconnected, when one person is empowered we are all impacted. When we respond with jealousy or resentment, we slow down our own progress; when we respond with joy and encouragement, we speed up our own progress as well as all others.

One of the most important contributions we can make to a group or an organization is to cheer and applaud those who are empowered. We can offer this feedback in private and in front of others at meetings. The more we notice what we appreciate and the more we acknowledge our appreciation to each other, the more the desired condition will show itself. Let us welcome the time when so many of us are empowered that parts of this book are obsolete.

In the next chapter, we focus on techniques -- mechanics -- that are available to assist at meetings to promote active participation and empowerment.

Chapter 7

Meeting Mechanics

Here are several helpful principles and techniques for attending to the mechanical aspects of your meeting. Included here are an explanation of the distinction between group content and process; information about developing ground rules; an outline of group decision-making methods; techniques for centering, brainstorming, and buzz groups; and questions for keeping groups on target. The last section is a questionnaire that you or your meeting participants can use to analyze the meeting.

Group Content and Process

An effective group attends to both content (or task) and process with an over-arching intention of empowering individuals and the group as a whole. Many groups pay attention to the content or task they must accomplish, yet have little awareness of the ways in which they accomplish it. Other groups are so focused on the process that they lose sight of the content.

Weaving all elements of group effectiveness into a balanced experience is a joyous art. Energy flows in a group when the content and process are attended to in proper proportion.

Content describes _what_ is to be accomplished. Other names for content are task, topic, project, subject matter, goal, assignment. The content may be directed by leadership from above or suggested by a meeting participant or mandated by a constituency.

A considerable amount of time may be spent in determining the goal or defining the assignment before time can be spent in accomplishing the task. Front-end quality time usually reaps benefits in the later results.

Content functions and roles include a myriad of actions. Some of these are: initiating and establishing goals and procedures, expressing opinions, clarifying facts, defining terms, offering suggestions, testing ideas, summarizing discussions and decisions, analyzing solutions.

Process describes _how_ the task or content is accomplished. Examples of process include how individuals interact and communicate with each other, how decisions are made, how procedures are carried out, and how conflicts are managed.

Process functions and roles include a myriad of actions. Some of these are: keeping open channels of communication, reducing tension, suggesting methods that promote participant sharing of comments and experiences, showing empathy, valuing contributions of others, reconciling differences, contributing observations about the process, evaluating group process, keeping time, pacing the group.

Ground Rules

Your group needs to determine its unique set of ground rules. Some groups may prefer to call these "rules" or "expectations" or "norms." Use the label that is appropriate for your group. It is helpful to have the most important ones stated explicitly.

Leaders of new groups may find it helpful to be ready to ask the group participants what ground rules they wish to adopt. Experienced leaders who have strong feelings may suggest specific ground rules to start a group in establishing its own.

For example, a leader or facilitator or participant may ask the group, "What ground rules shall we establish for smoking?" Or the leader may say, "As you know, we can't smoke in here. There's a smoking room at the end of the hall. We'll take a break about half way through."

Here are a few items that groups consider for ground rules: respect, confidentiality, agenda setting, listening, interruptions, speaking time limits, taking breaks, and items listed in Chapter 3 in Considerations for Groups. Ground rules often develop as a result of a resolved or unresolved conflict.

Common sense leads us to the right issues to discuss or decide in order to set ground rules. A new group may not know the norms it wants to live with until the group participants have history with each other.

Group Decision-Making Methods

The old paradigm of "majority rules" is still an option for some groups. Many groups use it only as a last resort. When we want to build healthy relationships among meeting participants we have decision-making options that tend to be more helpful than majority rule. These processes usually also yield better decisions.

It is most helpful and empowering when the group knows in advance which decision-making method or methods are to be used. Ideally, the group itself decides on the decision-making method.

Consensus

Consensus decisions are made by the acceptance of the group members. While not everyone needs to "agree" with the final decision, everyone does "accept" it. Consensus is in alignment with parliamentary procedures that states that group members must have the opportunity to object. Hearing no objection, the group can assume acceptance.

This is the method that is encouraged most of the time when the group wants to create feelings of belonging and on-going commitment. No winners and losers are identified by consensus. The group owns the decision. While consensus may seem to take longer, a group does improve with practice so that over time, it is both efficient and effective.

Group Rules with Leader or Participant Veto Option

This method allows group members to direct the decisions, with the leader or a participant maintaining the right to negate the general agreement of the members. Caution is made to any leader who uses this: use rarely, as it establishes a distrust in the integrity of the group. Managers in organizations are the most likely leaders to use this option.

Leader Rules

This method allows the leader to decide. When used most effectively, all roles are clear: the leader seeks the opinions and advice of the group, perhaps a subcommittee or advisory council, and then decides. A misuse of this method is to say or imply that the group has the responsibility to decide and then the leader takes over that responsibility.

Majority Rule by Voting

A classic principle of parliamentary procedures is that half the group members plus one decide. It follows that half the group members less one lose. Majority rule is more efficient in the short term than consensus, especially in large groups and groups of people who do not know each other well. Balance efficiency with building relationships to determine the appropriate time to use majority rule. Even the most effectively-run consensus groups may have to resort to voting from time to time.

Ranking (A Variation of Voting)

This method assigns numerical values to issues to be decided. It helps to place items in priority order. Ranking can be used to make a decision or to generate information to make a decision using another decision-making method.

Centering: Purpose and Phrases

From time to time, participants in a group may seem off-center or imbalanced. Too much chatter or arguing or confusion can create such a condition in an individual or the group as a whole.

A strategy called "centering" can assist a group in staying balanced. Centering focuses the energy so that it is used more efficiently. One of the simplest centering techniques is to become conscious of breathing. When we focus on our breathing, we turn the attention inward, the direction of our center.

Centering is especially effective at the beginning of a meeting because it sets the stage for balance and assists in tapping into the group's intention and deep source of energy. Of course, anytime the group seems to be off balance is the perfect time to suggest centering.

Here are a few ways to talk about incorporating centering into your meetings. You may feel you have more influence when you are in an official leadership role. However, these approaches or comments can be just as effective and sometimes even *more* effective when introduced by a group member.

"Before we begin today's meeting, let's take a few deep breaths and relax. Then we can all start refreshed."

"Let's take a few moments in silence to consider the topic(s) on our agenda."

"I know you all have a lot to say about this subject. Before we start talking, though, let's just have some quiet time."

"The intention each of us has established for this meeting is *so* important. Please take a few moments to connect with your own intention."

"This topic is important and I want to be certain that we don't just stay on the surface. So let's take a little time to open to the deeper issues silently. I'll let you know when it's time for discussion."

"I need a little time to explore what I really think (feel) about this. Can we just sit for a moment with our own thoughts (feelings)?"

"I can tell that many of you are burning to say something about this. Before we start speaking, let's take a few minutes to write down some of our ideas. After writing for three minutes, I'm going to suggest that you identify the most important idea you have on your list. Then we'll talk."

"I know we've all come today from many different directions and responsibilities. Let's take time to be fully present and let go of all the other stuff. Just relax and close your eyes for a few moments."

"I want to start our meeting in a relaxed and peaceful way. Here is some calming music, so just sit back and relax for a few minutes."

"I have a video to start off today's meeting. It has beautiful nature photography to help us feel in greater harmony."

Buzz Groups

To add variety and increase efficiency at a large meeting, subgroups can be formed. One special type of subgroup is the "buzz" group. Buzz groups are usually composed of about three to five persons who are quickly subdivided from the total group to discuss a specific topic, with or without a leader.

As with any subgroup, the greatest advantage of the buzz group is that more individuals are willing and able to participate than in a large group in the same amount of time. Buzz groups are randomly organized to pool ideas, solutions, and/or reactions. A spokesperson is sometimes chosen to summarize the discussion to the larger group.

Here are some of the advantages of using buzz groups at meetings. Buzz groups

- Support the principles of adult learning, which are based on self-responsibility, respect for the individual's life experiences and opinions, and active participation.

- Allow many group members to participate actively at the same time.

- Improve comprehension and commitment because participants are actively involved and can experiment with ideas.

- Allow participants to connect with each other in a way that is not possible in a large group.

- Enrich later sharing in the total group because many individuals have tested their ideas.

- Shift the energy away from one central focus or person.

- Allow leader(s) to assign different small tasks so that the total group can cover an entire project.

- Vary the pace and action of a meeting.

- Help group members to get to know each other more easily than in the larger group.

- Revitalize a meeting.

- Increase group synergy, enthusiasm, and commitment.

- Provide a safe opportunity to test and experiment with new ideas and/or skills.

- Equalize participation so that the quick and experienced group members do not overwhelm or discourage the slower and less experienced participants.

- Create a sense of ownership of the final objectives, conclusion, or learning.

Brainstorming

Brainstorming is a popular, efficient method of generating many ideas so that the most useful ones can be exposed and explored. By applying strict rules while generating many ideas, the discussion that follows is greatly enhanced.

When discussion and judgment of ideas occur during the brainstorming process, valuable energy is lost. Group members are less likely to offer additional ideas if earlier ones are attacked. When ideas are allowed to flow without discouragement, synergy occurs.

Recording ideas is essential so that the group can have an overview of all its ideas. Typically, the most obvious ideas emerge first. Since some of the best ideas emerge after a silence, it is helpful to avoid intervening just to fill the moment with sound. Generally, brainstorming is lively, but a slow pace can be just as valuable, especially when the topic or problem is challenging or complex.

After accumulating many ideas, qualifying and analyzing them are important. With a large list of ideas recorded on a chalkboard or flip chart, group members can easily see and select the most relevant ones. Impractical ideas usually drop away, with little time used for discussion.

Here is an acronym to assist in remembering the general rules of brainstorming.

Ideas by Brainstorming

Ideas are recorded for later reference.

Delay discussing, agreeing, or disagreeing with ideas.

Expand and hitchhike on others' ideas.

Abbreviate thoughts to record ideas quickly.

Strive for quantity of ideas; quality can come later.

Keeping Groups on Target

Here are some questions to assist you in keeping groups on target, on the goal. If members of your group have a tendency to not follow through, you can ask these questions out loud at the time of the goal setting to increase the likelihood that commitments will be kept.

WHAT?
- What is the goal?
  - Is it specific?
  - Is it measurable?
  - Is it attainable?
  - Is it what we really want to accomplish?
  - Is it worthy of our attention?
- What do we need to know or explore?
- What feelings do we have about the goal?

HOW?
- How will we achieve the goal?
- How can we generate or maintain enthusiasm?
- How will we demonstrate we have achieved the goal?

WHO?
- Who is excited about the goal?
- Who will be responsible?
- Who else is involved?
- Who is the audience?
- Who must be informed?
- Who can help? Who may hinder?

WHEN?
- By when must we achieve the goal?
- When are the intermediary steps or deadlines, if any?
- When do we return to the group with a problem?

Analyzing a Meeting Afterward

This set of questions assists in analyzing the effectiveness of a meeting. It can be used as a guide to assessing meetings personally or as a guide to discussion among group members.

LEADERSHIP:
- Was leader clear about task and process?
- Did leader encourage everyone to participate? How?
- How did leader relate to group members?

PARTICIPATION:
- Did you participate? Did others participate?
- Did members show they listened to each other? How?
- Did you feel included or excluded?

INFORMATION:
- How was information collected from or given to the group?
- Was this process effective?
- Was the information valuable and relevant?

DECISIONS:
- How were decisions made?
- Was there agreement? Disagreement?
- How committed are members to the decisions?

ENERGY:
- How do you describe the energy in the group?
- Would more be accomplished if the energy were different?
- How was the energy different at different times?

SATISFACTION:
- How do you rate your satisfaction?
  With the process?
  With decisions?
  With the leader?
  With the group?
  With the results?
  With your own involvement?
- How satisfied do you believe others are?

CHANGES:
- What changes do you want in the future?
- What suggestions can you offer to others?
- How can you change yourself to enhance future meetings?

EMPOWERMENT:
- Do you feel empowered?
- Were there times when you felt disempowered?
  What was that like?
  How did (or will) you get your power back?
- Do you believe others are empowered?
  What leads you to believe what you believe?
  Can you assist someone to feel empowered?

FOLLOW UP:
- What provisions have been made for follow up?
- Do you believe everyone will follow through on commitments?
- How can you enhance the probability for greater follow up?

Meeting Mechanics at Work

While we do not want to reduce the interactions at meetings to mere "mechanics," it is helpful to know that certain mechanisms and tools are available to us. The techniques mentioned specifically in this chapter are suggestive of still others that are not specifically described here. You will find yourself expanding into more and more empowering ways of being at meetings as you explore and experiment.

The techniques in this chapter work effectively, until they do *not* work. That is, they are tested and proven approaches based on solid principles. All things change. Things *must* change; life is dynamic. Today you can select from the tools available and make a new selection tomorrow and yet another next month. And you can invent new tools. As Abraham Maslow said, "If the only tool you have is a hammer, every problem is a nail."

In the next section we open your tool box still wider. We offer more principles and techniques on energetics and empowerment through the experience of difficult behavior and other challenges.

Handling Difficult Behavior

Good intentions, empowerment tools, skills at meeting mechanics, and the ability to work well with interpersonal relations enhance the probability of energetic and meaningful meetings. Challenges might still arise.

This section provides options, suggestions, and techniques for dealing with situations that occur even though the group has organized itself to prevent difficulties. Out of differences arise conflicts, which must be managed. Pain from the past or present must be healed when it comes into awareness.

Chapter 8 focuses on principles and techniques for energetic release. Included are powerful tools that introduce you to transforming dense or dysfunctional energetic conditions so that meetings can be more effective.

Chapter 9 defines difficult behavior and lays the foundation for the next chapter. Chapter 10 lists twenty-two behavior patterns, possible motivations for these patterns, and a variety of actions to assist in transforming the behavior that is considered difficult.

Chapter 11 focuses on transforming the difficult behavior covered in chapters 9 and 10 into empowerment. The New Meeting Paradigm is described in this ending chapter. Or is it a beginning? For every end there is a beginning; every beginning, an end.

Chapter 8

Energetic Release

Pollution in the Energy Field

Difficult behavior pollutes the energy field. Difficult behavior can also occur *because* the energy field is polluted. As we become more and more attentive to energy and energetics, we come to understand the impact of energetic pollution on ourselves and others.

Pollution in the energy field causes discomfort and disease, as polluted air and water cause discomfort and disease. Sensitive persons are especially susceptible to toxicity. Some individuals can live in a polluted environment for a long time without noticing its condition or feeling negative results. Many do not associate discomfort with a polluted energy field.

With high intention, energy can be aligned so that pollution and pain lift easily. The willingness to release pain or toxicity can come from one individual, but it is far more efficient and effective when the group participants decide to work together to transform the flow of energy.

When pollution is trapped in the energy field of a room or a large group, it is not necessary to ask the group's permission to clear it. When we enter a room before a meeting and discover dirty ashtrays from the previous group, we would not ask permission of the incoming group to clean the ashtrays. We simply empty the ashtrays. Or maybe we choose not to clean the mess, but we certainly do not ask permission.

High Intention

Entering the energy field of an individual or a cohesive group without permission is a different matter. This can be invasive. When possible, we ask permission. Otherwise, we work with high intention. This requires letting go of the belief that we know the appropriate outcome. A general, all-purpose, generic high intention is "My intention is that the energy flow in a way that serves the highest good of all."

Individuals newly aware of energy work -- especially the *power* of energy work -- often make an observation that it seems manipulative. The concern expressed is usually that energy work is *inappropriate* because it is manipulative.

Manipulation happens constantly in our culture, usually without high intention. Advertising, marketing, most organizations, and most relationships are organized to manipulate someone or something. If we keep our intention clear (e.g., for the highest good of all) and let go of believing we that know the solution for others, we take giant leaps into new ways of being in the world. Other high intentions to live by are "to do no harm" and "to make a positive difference wherever I go."

Releasing the Pain in Your Group

Energetic release work clears the maximum pain with minimal discomfort. Pain exists at the surface of our experiences. When we stuff that pain inward, it gets compacted. The density of this stuffed pain can be so great that most people do not want to work through it. That is understandable; it is painful!

Pain results from unresolved interpersonal issues, from disappointments in jobs or projects, from individuals who are no longer part of the group, and from fears associated with internal and external factors. The reason for the pain is not nearly as important as the way the pain is managed. When it is managed poorly, especially over time, it takes a toll. Eventually everyone can be harmed by the pain, including those not involved directly with the original situation.

Generally, it is not the responsibility of group leaders to work through unresolved interpersonal issues, grief, or deep-seated fears. This is best left with trained professional therapists. Keep in mind, though, that the pain or pollution associated with these issues is in the energy field and impacts everyone. Dismissing it as "not mine" or "not appropriate to work through" is a form of unhealthy denial.

When we know that with high intention and simple techniques we can clear a polluted energy field, we have an obligation to do so, for our own health and the health of others. If we do not notice, then we have no obligation. Consciousness and responsibility are connected.

There are many techniques and principles related to releasing pain energetically. The principles are more important, but sometimes harder to grasp, than the techniques. When we embody the principles, clear intention can yield results without any techniques at all.

This is a principle: *We can identify, neutralize, and lift pain energetically.* Many techniques can achieve this goal; for example, we can use imagery. First, we identify the pain in a tangible way: *it's sharp, like a nail.* Then we work with the characteristics by imagining a change: *soften the sharpness, remove the nail.* The pain lifts.

Working directly with the energetics of the pain (qualities such as sharpness; images such as a nail) is far more efficient than working through why the nail is there. Years can be required to determine why the nail got there using traditional methods. Only seconds are needed to lift the pain when the nail is ready to release. If the nail does not instantly release, it is not ready, and must be approached in other ways, including more traditional methods. Energetic release work is deep, gentle, lasting, and fast. Dealing only with content or history slows down the healing.

Here is an example: *at a meeting, Jim reports on a project he manages. He admits it is troublesome and even indicates that he has pains in his stomach as a result of the problems. Then suddenly he feels better -- hurray! But Andrea, sitting on the other side of the room, suddenly feels pain. She says it feels like a belt has tightened around her waist. The pain is intense.*

I ask if she can see a belt in her mind's eye. When she says "yes," I ask her to describe it. "It's black....leather...tight, very tight....It has a big brass buckle." I instruct her to unbuckle the belt and let it drop to the floor. It dissolves so that no one else can take it on.

Several persons in the group sigh in great relief when they realize they feel lighter. The pain is gone from the energy field. One week later, still no pain. Jim has rediscovered his enthusiasm for the project and feels no pains in his stomach.

Much happens in the invisible world. We sensitive humans do not invent the invisible world; we observe it and work with it. The invisible world is a realm of reality different from the physical reality. As we learn to have greater mastery over the physical world, we also have greater insights into the invisible or energetic world.

Pain is separation, below which is fear. The energy of fear vibrates intensively and acts as a magnet for the very experiences we fear and claim we do not want. So here is a recipe: *extract the intensity of the energy of the fear. Discard the fear. Feel the intensity you have just extracted, letting it energize the image of the experience you want. Sprinkle with joy. Simmer for as long as you want. Enjoy.*

Here is a fear expressed in words: *"I'm afraid I'll lose my job. Then I won't have money to pay the mortgage or send my kids to college. At my age I'll have trouble finding another job."*

Here is the above fear expressed energetically: *Weight on shoulders. Knot in pit of stomach. Cloud of darkness all around person. Knife in back. Off balance, as if to stumble. Heaviness.*

The fear expressed in words can continue for hours or even months, as one mulls over the circumstances, feeling victimized. Working energetically, however, we can lift off the accumulation of "stuff" so that clearer thinking can occur. A shift of consciousness can occur faster and more deeply when we work with the energy field.

After an upward shift in consciousness, the words describing the situation may sound like this, *"I'm excited about the challenges here. I know that when it's time for me to work somewhere else, I'll be excited about that, also. My wonderful kids are going to have a meaningful college experience, I know that for certain. I feel as much joy when I'm at home as when I'm here at the office. All is well."*

Energetically, the shift may present itself like this: *Lightness surrounds the person. Energy flows smoothly throughout the body. Vitality. Buoyancy. Body organs sing in perfect harmony. Knowingness of being in the right place at the right time. Calmness.*

This is *not* simply positive thinking, although a positive mental attitude is certainly an appropriate starting place. Deep transformation requires a shift in consciousness, deeper than the thinking level. The energy changes. The energy field changes.

Maintaining the same level of energetic *intensity* when in joy or deep satisfaction as when in fear is the challenge. People often discount an experience of joy or spiritual enlightenment as perhaps an isolated event or even fiction created by the imagination. After the excitement of the experience has left, we often return to familiar patterns. Fear may be part of that familiar pattern.

The Focus of Our Attention Expands

As we give our attention to an idea or a thing, we give it our energy and our consciousness. As we continue to give this thing our attention, it increases in our awareness. Indeed, it expands. Persons who constantly give their attention to the negative expand their awareness to see even more negativity. Persons who constantly give their attention to the positive expand their awareness to see even more positiveness.

When we do not want something in our lives, it is wise to not give that thing too much attention, as we will expand that thing in our consciousness. Instead, it is wise to invest our attention in the idea or thing that we want to receive or experience. It is wise to invest our attention in what we want, not what we do not want. It is empowering to invest our attention in what is right, not what is wrong.

Many individuals focus primarily on what is wrong in a situation: the grammatical error in a report, the flip chart diagram that is messy, or the leader who makes a mistake. When our primary intention is to find what is *wrong*, our eyes rarely fail us. However, when our primary intention is to focus on what is *right*, we see errors and mistakes differently. We see them as a opportunity to learn discernment -- a way to heighten appreciation for meaningful life experiences.

Here is an example. Andrew and Tim are both production supervisors in a small manufacturing firm, reporting to the plant manager, Rod. Andrew and Tim work well together on various product lines. Both are in their early 30's and considered smart and successful in supervising their respective small team of employees. They get along well with the other supervisors. And here end the similarities and harmony.

Andrew is frustrated because Rod's management style annoys him; at times, Andrew confronts Rod with his criticism. He feels disempowered. By contrast, Tim notices Rod's management style is different from his own and is sometimes frustrated by Rod's decisions or manner. Tim recognizes that Rod is the manager because he knows the business and has a good track record. Tim feels that more work will be accomplished by maintaining good relations with Rod.

At staff meetings, Andrew makes comments about the "bad" coffee. Tim does not like the coffee, either, but brings his own or goes without. Andrew takes every opportunity to point out errors he sees, especially when Rod makes them. Tim is just as aware of errors, but acts out his discernment by asking helpful questions or looking for solutions or next steps.

Andrew believes that it is important to mention everything that is wrong to avoid bigger problems later. Tim believes that it is important to notice what is wrong so that creative solutions can be found as soon as possible.

Often, Andrew focuses his attention so much on what is wrong that he often cannot or will not see what is right. Tim can redirect his attention from what is wrong to what is right and hold the two in balance.

Andrew is creating a negative pool of energy around himself. Tim's energy field is clearer and cleaner. If Andrew is to continue in this manner, he is likely to create a considerable amount of animosity among his peers and even his subordinates. When the opportunity for promotion opens up, Andrew is unlikely to be considered unless he changes his ways.

Creating Energetic Waste

Recycling and proper disposal of both reusable and toxic material waste are hot topics right now in our culture -- especially among those who are concerned with the environment. Conscience stirs many to act. Laws and regulations stimulate others to act. Accessible and visible recycling containers help to raise the consciousness for treating our planet with respect and love.

Energetic clearing requires the constant recycling of energy -- finding new ways to use "stuff" that is no longer useful in the old context or in the familiar way. Since everything is energy, we do not really "get rid" of anything, we transform it. We change its form. Ideally, we transform it into something that benefits someone, perhaps ourselves.

Some forms of energy we see, touch, taste, hear, or smell. These forms are familiar, but forms in the nonphysical world are no less real; they are simply in another dimension of reality. One dimension is not "better" than another; it is simply different.

Energetic clearing processes produce "waste" as do processes that are not necessarily considered "energetic clearing." For example, organizational consultants, psychologists, managers, and group leaders are in positions to help others in their growth and learning. When we grow into something we grow out of something else.

When helpers help, they can stir up "stuff" which needs to be treated as waste. The stuff may be words or emotions or actions, all of which are and have energy. This is waste that can be used or recycled. If it is not used or recycled, it clogs the system.

Disposing of Energetic Waste

Where does this stuff go? What happens to it? We have all had a difficult challenge and then dumped the toxicity of the challenge elsewhere. A classic example is: a problem at work or in a meeting is dumped on the family that evening. Sometimes we do not realize what we are doing. Usually we do not intend to hurt someone we love because the boss is critical or a meeting is frustrating.

We need to be responsible about the way in which we dispose of this energetic waste. It is toxic. Most of us try to be responsible. We avoid or try to avoid over-reacting with our family when work is stressful, for example. The more conscious we are of our emotions and thoughts, the more attentive we are to channeling the energy that is propelled by the emotions and thoughts.

Even sincere determination to be appropriate may not be enough to direct certain forms of toxic energetic waste. This waste can leak without our awareness. Recycling bins in the energy field are effective, but are not always perceived. Other techniques that are even more powerful are included later in this chapter.

Times are Changing

Many helping professionals are proficient by normal standards; some have been proficient for a long time. However, times are changing. Everything is changing. Practices must change, too. Practices can change intentionally. If not, they become first ineffective and then destructive. (So, you see, they change, anyway.) Practitioners in many disciplines begin to *add* to the problem of their clients when their practices do not reflect an upward shift in consciousness.

We can choose to change. Or we can just change. Popular is the expression, "We'll change when we're ready." Nonsense! We change all the time. And we are *not* always ready. Even those who are ready and eager for change may not always be ready for the change that happens.

This is a time for transformation. As we transform, we generate energy that must be used. The more constructive that use of energy, the faster humanity shifts from a belief in toxicity and illness to a belief in lightness and wholeness. It is time for moving the attention of our faith from the outer effects to the inner wisdom.

Constructive Use of Toxic Energetic Waste

Farmers know that when manure is spread around properly it becomes fertilizer. When it just sits, it is excrement, waste. So, too, with *energetic* waste. It needs to be spread around, put to use.

Emotions are energy. Anger is a normal human emotion. When properly used, it motivates. The three-year-old child who yells when her fire truck catches on the rug blows off steam in a normal way. She pulls harder on the truck. When the screaming is done, the anger is done. This burst of energy propels her into solving her problem.

As that child grows, she learns to handle anger in other ways. She probably learns that it is not appropriate to blow off steam or that she must learn to control her temper. Her family or other social institutions explain or model for her the cultural restrictions. Her normal anger is likely to build or fester. Psychologists talk about repressed or suppressed emotions, phobias, denials. The list of labels is long.

Energy that once burst from her now compacts or leaks from her. The energetic waste builds as she talks about her unhappy childhood or more recent woes. When she repeatedly tells her story, energetic waste accumulates still more or leaks on her listeners.

As an adult, this three-year-old child with the fire truck needs to manage built-up anger that she has forgotten how to release spontaneously. This energy no longer propels her, it slows her down and even sickens her. The energy is discernible and moveable. She does not have to keep talking about all the injustices in her life to heal herself. All she has to do is identify the energy and transform it. The transformation is accelerated when there is a specific place to move the energy.

Techniques for Proper Disposal of Energetic Waste

Everything that exists in the physical, emotional, mental, or spiritual aspects has an energy field. When we become sensitive to energy, we master a great power that we can use in many ways. It is not necessary to see or feel the energy; even *imagining* the possibility that a power exists in the invisible realms can be transformational.

Here are several techniques that are especially helpful before, during, and after meetings.

Clockwise Upward Spiral

This technique is recommended for managers, trainers, group leaders, consultants, and anyone in charge of group meetings.

Prior to the meeting, see or imagine that you see energy moving around the room in a clockwise direction, gently spiraling upward. The pace can vary. With greater use, many layers of energy move at a variety of speeds when the upward spiral is envisioned.

During the meeting, activate the Spiral, especially if there is any difficulty. Disagreements and tempers and confusion all tend to move in a counterclockwise direction. These dynamics respond well to the intentional clockwise movement and the upward spiraling direction.

After the meeting, clear the room by using this Clockwise Upward Spiral. Consider this similar to disposing of dirty cups and crumpled note paper. Energy clearing work is easier than removing physical waste. It can even be done after you have left the room, if necessary.

After this Spiral is in place, -- with three to ten activations -- it will operate on its own. It is helpful to continue to check the Spiral from time to time, especially if the room is used for many meetings. Expect meetings to run more smoothly, since groups no longer have to deal with the toxic residue from past gatherings. As conflict is expressed in current meetings, the Spiral lifts it so that it does not weigh down other interactions. Keep checking the Spiral from time to time.

Cutting Negative Bonds of Attachment

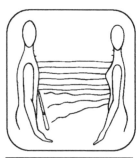

Negative Bonds of Attachment*

This technique is recommended if you are attached negatively to someone. Relationships with emotional aspects often have negative attachments. Negative bonds with one person can impact *all* other relationships. While most effective when guided by an experienced facilitator, it can be done on your own or with someone not experienced by following these guidelines.

Set an intention to cut negative bonds that attach you with someone. Make it as high as possible, for example, *To assist us in clear, honest communications.* Be certain you are ready for this disengagement. Positive bonds between you and the person will *not* be cut.

Close your eyes and relax. Bring into your awareness the person to whom you are negatively attached. See or imagine that you see a cord connecting the two of you. Where is it attached on you? How big is it? How else might you describe it?

In your inner awareness, ask the other person if he or she wishes to have the cord cut. If your intuition tells you no, cut your end of the cord *only* and hand it to the person's higher self, lovingly. The person's higher self is that part of him or her that has greater consciousness than the ordinary self. If your intuition tells you that the person's higher self wants the cord cut, cut your end of the cord first and then the other end.

Whether you cut both ends or only one, bring to your imagination the proper cutting instrument: wire cutters for wire, scissors for string, a blow torch for metal piping. Allow the cord or wire or string to lift into the light. Imagine soothing energy dropping into the cut area(s). If you feel exhausted after this process, rest. It is similar to a surgical procedure.

If there are others to whom you are negatively attached, repeat the process. Do not try to cut cords from different persons at the same time. You could end up in a tangled mess.

* From *Symbolic Language of Energy* by Jeanie Marshall

Bundling Waste

This technique requires us to recognize that we are releasing toxicity. The toxic release may be anger we aimed at a group leader yesterday or rage that wells up in us when we remember how one of our parents treated us when we were six years old.

We imagine that the toxicity has density, shape, and color. There is no need to analyze it, only identify and imagine it. We pull the density from our body. In our mind's eye, we put it in a bundle -- a plain paper wrapper or a burlap sack or whatever we like. We toss it upward, into the ethers, letting angelic helpers catch it and put it to good use.

We applaud ourselves for letting this stuff go and for making it available to be used constructively in other dimensions. Remember that all energy can be recycled. When we hold onto it, though, we can keep ourselves stuck.

This technique works days or even years after the experience that stimulated the toxic energy. We can go back and haul away the trash from the past. There is no limitation of time or space when working in the energy field. The only time is **NOW**.

Deep Breathing

Here is the simplest technique of all. All we need is with us every moment: our breath! No one needs to know that we are doing anything out of the ordinary.

When we feel distressed, we can easily breathe the discomfort away. And we can avoid some distress by taking a few deep breaths at various times throughout the day. The deep breaths allow oxygen to flow into our system and relax us. Energetically, the breaths center and balance us. It is important to not underestimate the power of this simple technique. Breathe! Breathe deeper!

Triangles in a Meeting

The triangle is a powerful form. Energy is intensified around the points of the triangle. In a meeting, individuals form triangles of energy. Every three persons form a triangle, and each of those persons forms triangles with all others in the group, and so on.

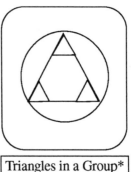

Triangles in a Group*

Energetic release can be accelerated when these triangles are established with high intention. Individuals are connected heart to heart for the most gentle deep release. It is helpful to envision three empowered persons as the "base" triangle.

Below are the number of distinct triangles that can be formed according to the number of persons at your meeting, up to 50 persons. This illustrates the power of focused groups as we observe the exponential increase for each additional person

3	1	19	969	35	6545
4	4	20	1140	36	7140
5	10	21	1330	37	7770
6	20	22	1540	38	8436
7	35	23	1771	39	9139
8	56	24	2024	40	9880
9	84	25	2300	41	10660
10	120	26	2600	42	11480
11	165	27	2925	43	12341
12	220	28	3276	44	13244
13	286	29	3654	45	14190
14	364	30	4060	46	15180
15	455	31	4495	47	16215
16	560	32	4960	48	17296
17	680	33	5456	49	18424
18	816	34	5984	50	19600

* From *Symbolic Language of Energy* by Jeanie Marshall

Energetic Release at Work

And we have only touched the surface of the ways in which we can release toxicity from the energy field. Thousands of techniques and energetic forms and models are available to us. I personally have used hundreds and each reader has used other hundreds.

Yet when we sort out all the methods, the one that comes to the top of the list is not a technique at all, but a life style: to live with high intention. You may call this intention love or joy or peace or open communications. Living with high intention produces miracles in all our experiences.

When we are surrounded with loving, high-intentioned others, it is easier to live in high intention. The *test* is to remain or move into living with high intention when confronted by those whose behavior we consider to be problematic. The following chapters address difficult behavior and empowering ways to respond to it.

Chapter 9

Difficult Behavior

What is Difficult Behavior?

A behavior that is difficult for one person may be child's play for another. A behavior that is difficult for one person at one time may be delightful another time. A behavior that is difficult in one situation may be easy in another.

When discussing difficult behavior, it is important to stay focused on the behavior or the action or the words that are spoken. Many people have a tendency to apply an adjective to a person, labeling the person difficult. For example, one may exhibit dominant behavior, yet we prefer to avoid calling the person "dominant." A behavior is easier to transform than a personality trait, perceived or real. Therefore, it is more appropriate to give our attention to behavior than personality.

Leaders and others who work with persons at meetings need to be attentive to describing behavior without resorting to labeling individuals. Labels can keep people in boxes. If we hold a vision that someone is a "rambler," our vision can be a stumbling block for the person to act any way other than how we see him or her; that is, rambling.

Even the term "difficult behavior" is not the most empowering designation. However, it gets the attention of group participants and serves as a bridge to more constructive behavior and approaches.

Considering Difficult Behavior and You

You may want to consider what behavior, in particular, causes you difficulty. You may find it helpful to remind yourself of the persons who have demonstrated that behavior. Then -- and this may be the hardest part -- reflect on your *own* actions and reactions.

Consider how you may contribute to the behavior in others that challenges you. Perhaps something in your style elicits the difficult behavior in others. Perhaps not. For example, if you tend to be quick to respond, you may find that persons around you are quiet, a behavior which annoys you. Or perhaps others are inspired by your quickness and find their own passion, challenging you with talkativeness.

Consider, what in you is similar to the behavior you find especially difficult. For example, if persons who refuse to budge from a position really bother you, consider if you use stubborn behavior in situations. Or, if you find dominant behavior annoying, consider if you might sometimes dominate meetings or relationships in other settings.

Watch and consider how you impact others, especially those whose behavior you find difficult. As you watch yourself, you may find it particularly helpful to move from reflecting in the first person to reflecting in the third person, calling yourself by name.

Here is an example about Mary's experience with Kevin. The first person account might be: "I get so frustrated when Kevin interrupts me at staff meetings." The third person account might be: "Mary gets frustrated when Kevin interrupts her at staff meetings." Reading this on the written page in a book might make this strategy appear to be more like a gimmick than a transformational tool. However, you can learn mastery by witnessing your own behavior.

Consider right now your own reactions to a recent situation when you were challenged by difficult behavior -- your own or someone else's. Recount the memory in the first person, e.g., "I felt.... Then I said ...." Then, tell the story to yourself again, but this time in the third person, as if someone else were talking about how you felt and what you said.

Then notice the differences between the two approaches. The differences may be subtle. If they are too subtle to notice on the first attempt, simply experiment again. You will be empowered by what you can learn about yourself in a short period of time using this method of witnessing your thoughts, feelings, behavior, and words.

Consider, also, what you can learn about yourself and life from a situation that is difficult and from the person who is exhibiting difficult behavior. Every situation has a gift in it. The sooner you receive the gift, the sooner you are freed from the situation that haunts you.

Difficult Behavior and Conflict

For many individuals, there is a definite relationship between difficult behavior and conflict. With both, the degree of intensity and the proximity of the situation are relevant to our perceptions, tolerance, and feelings.

At times, we will want to detach ourselves, as suggested by the above approach to witnessing our experiences. At other times, it will be more important to go deeper into the situation to understand it and to capture all the growth opportunities. This can sometimes be messy and even grueling. Each situation offers you choices.

The windows through which we view conflicts are crucial to the way in which we see them. Seeing conflicts through a window of fear shows us dynamics that are fearful and uncomfortable. Seeing conflicts as situations to be avoided -- perhaps at any cost -- will not necessarily eliminate conflicts, and will, perhaps, prove to be very costly.

Seeing conflicts as the manifestation of differences allows us greater access to the energy and creativity that can come from those differences. Seeing conflicts as an opportunity to find creative solutions leads us to the creative solutions because those are what we seek. Life is an extraordinary series of opportunities that allows us to choose how to frame the pictures we see.

Assessing a Conflict

On the facing page is a matrix created by a simple cost-benefit analysis to help you assess a conflict. In the boxes created by the elements, list the responses to the following questions.

- **Identify the unresolved conflict in a brief statement.**
    1. What is the statement to which those involved can agree?
    Is this situation worthy of your attention?

- **Consider information about continuing the conflict.**
    2. What are the costs to continuing the conflict?
    Costs to you, others, the group, the organization and/or society.
    Consider vitality and resources in addition to money, time.

    3. What are the benefits to continuing the conflict?
    Someone benefits or the conflict would not exist.
    Consider your own benefits and the benefits of all others.

    4. Who has the energy to continue the conflict?
    Do you? Do others?
    When does the energy run out?

- **Consider information about ending the conflict.**
    5. What are the costs to ending the conflict?
    Costs to you, others, the group, the organization and/or society.
    Consider vitality and resources in addition to money and time.

    6. What are the benefits to ending the conflict?
    Consider your own benefits and the benefits of all others.
    Someone has to benefit or the conflict will not end.

    7. Who has the energy to end the conflict?
    Do you? Do others?
    When does the energy run out?

- **Consider action steps.**
    8. As action steps become obvious, who will do what by when?
    What additional attention or energy will be required?

1. Conflict:

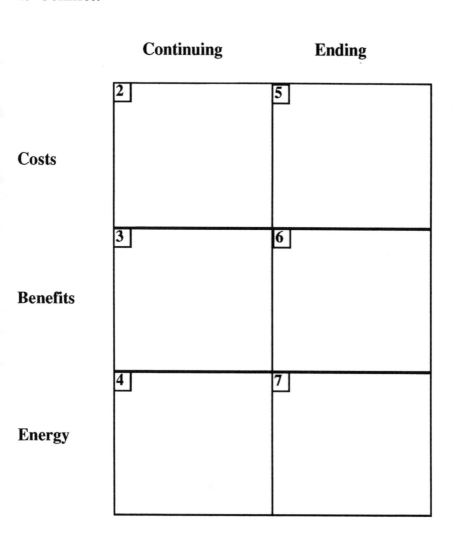

	Continuing	Ending
Costs	2	5
Benefits	3	6
Energy	4	7

8. Action:

Difficult Behavior at Work

Difficult behavior and other forms of conflict or challenges present us with opportunities. Without them, we would not, perhaps, have accomplished certain goals in our life. This dynamic is part of the old paradigm.

We can bless the obstacles without believing that we must always experience them in order to be successful. Whether we are overcome by obstacles or we are overcoming obstacles, we are still in the energy of "overcoming." Acting in ways that are difficult for others or reacting with resistance to others' difficult behavior puts us in the energy of "difficulty."

Certainly, our history has shown us it is important to be able to overcome obstacles when they are in our path. This can become such a habit that some individuals put obstacles in their path just so they can overcome them. When obstacles are *not* in our path, we must overcome overcoming.

Many of us can see the New Paradigm for business, families, communities, and, indeed, all relationships. Some of us have the courage to talk and write about this New Paradigm, which fosters a higher form of being than overcoming difficulty or trying to cope in an unfriendly world. In the New Paradigm, we allow ourselves to live in the present moment, whatever the present moment presents. We live from the power source that is inside us, without being changed by our outer environment. We see the world as friendly.

The next chapter identifies twenty-two difficult behaviors and empowering ideas for responding to them. The final chapter discusses the gifts of those behavior patterns as a path to empowerment.

Chapter 10

Difficult Behavior Patterns

Twenty-two Difficult Behavior Patterns

The list of twenty-two behavior patterns that follows has emerged from work with individuals in groups. A brief description of each behavior is listed at the top of the page. Leaders and participants must be constantly attentive to weighing the rights and needs of individuals with the rights and needs of the group as a whole.

In the left column is a list of possible motivations, which are not necessarily mutually exclusive. They are included to assist participants in recognizing that there is not only one possible reason for a behavior.

In the right column is a list of possible responses, which are also not necessarily exclusive. Suggestions listed in one behavior may also be helpful with another behavior. Standard procedures and prevention strategies, options for the current situation, and energetic considerations are included.

As you continue to work in groups at meetings, you will find that you have less and less need for specific techniques and more need to be totally present to the current situation. By "totally present" we mean to be in the "here and now," trusting your inner wisdom, acting from high intention, and giving your attention fully to the present situation, not one in the past or future.

List of Difficult Behavior Patterns

Behavior Patterns
that are
Aggressive or Attacking

Attacking behavior is disruptive to a group and can be a deterrent to participation and even attendance. The group as a whole has a responsibility to hold such behavior in check and use the energy of the attack in more constructive ways.

Some individuals act aggressively or attack on a regular basis, which may lead us to identify that person as "aggressive" or "attacking." However, we must be careful to focus on behavior rather than personality or labels. Most of us at some time in our lives will attack or act in aggressive, even hostile ways.

Leaders or other group members may believe that those who attack do not need protection. While our first instinct may be to protect the one(s) being attacked, it is important to remember that the one attacking may also need to be protected -- if not right now, later, when the energy of attack may reverse directions.

The energy field around those who are attacking is likely to be harsh. The aggressive or attacking energy tends to prompt from others either retreat or an equal force of energy, attacking back. Energy that is smooth or soft or calm is the most helpful when attacking behavior needs to be neutralized.

Empowered persons do not attack. They do not need to attack, they only need to allow their inner power to be expressed. Our job as leaders and group members is to assist everyone in being empowered.

Acts Passive Aggressively

Acts passive, but is really aggressive. The behavior -- verbal and/or nonverbal -- is often biting or snide.

POSSIBLE MOTIVATIONS	POSSIBLE ACTIONS FOR LEADER AND/OR OTHERS

POSSIBLE MOTIVATIONS

- *Is annoyed with one or more group members or with leader*
- *Feels personal needs are not being met*
- *Seems or is preoccupied with an issue outside the meeting scope*
- *Has a hidden agenda*
- *Wants to be center of attention*

POSSIBLE ACTIONS FOR LEADER AND/OR OTHERS

Standard Procedures/Prevention Strategies

- Structure the meeting so everyone focuses on agenda item rather than personalities.
- Allow members to express personal goals for group and/or the meeting.

Options for the Current Situation

- Inquire if the individual wishes to discuss a particular issue.
- Ignore the situation if it does not negatively affect you or the rest of the group.
- Use humor that encourages yet does not embarrass the individual.
- Confront the individual, if you are prepared to handle the response.
- Avoid arguing with the individual or trying to be a therapist.
- Discuss concerns privately with individual at break time, if all else fails.

Energetic Considerations

- Envision the smooth exchange of energy between this person and the group as a whole.

Argues

Fights with one or more others in the group or fights against the issues under discussion.

POSSIBLE MOTIVATIONS	POSSIBLE ACTIONS FOR LEADER AND/OR OTHERS

POSSIBLE MOTIVATIONS

- *Is naturally combative*
- *Is frustrated*
- *Feels his or her needs are not being addressed*
- *Is annoyed with one or more group members or with the leader*

POSSIBLE ACTIONS FOR LEADER AND/OR OTHERS

Standard Procedures/Prevention Strategies

- Be fair. Give *all* persons a chance to express opinions. Disruptive arguing will be less prevalent when differences are valued.
- Recognize that diversity in a group is healthy and helpful, so do not discourage all argument.

Options for the Current Situation

- Restate views so individual knows that she or he has been heard clearly.
- Designate a later time when subject can be discussed more fully.
- Find points that arguing sides have in common.
- Control your own temper and try to keep group members from getting overly excited.
- Identify positive and negative forces for the suggestions.
- Encourage group to respond to issues.
- Discuss concerns privately with individual at break time, if all else fails.

Energetic Considerations

- Envision the group as a symphony; this is a time of momentary disharmony.

Attacks Group or Individuals

Strikes out at one or more members of the group or the whole group either passive aggressively or violently.

POSSIBLE MOTIVATIONS	POSSIBLE ACTIONS FOR LEADER AND/OR OTHERS

POSSIBLE MOTIVATIONS

- *Is angry about something related or unrelated to this meeting*
- *Dislikes one or more group members or the leader*
- *Wants to embarrass, hurt, or "put down" others*
- *Finds group or meeting unresponsive to personal needs*
- *Is naturally aggressive or combative*

POSSIBLE ACTIONS FOR LEADER AND/OR OTHERS

Standard Procedures/Prevention Strategies

- Protect group and all its members, including the one on the attack.
- Envision a high intention for the group, for example, "For synergistic solutions with the highest good for all in mind."

Options for the Current Situation

- Direct or redirect comments to the issues or tasks on the agenda, away from personalities.
- Restate goal or current agenda item.
- Do *not* fight back.
- Lower your voice to achieve greater control and reduce the negative emotions.
- Acknowledge the individual's right to leave the meeting.
- Question the attacker's commitment to the goal.
- Say that you will not tolerate or collude with aggressive behavior.

Energetic Considerations

- Send attacker loving energy. This person does not need your anger or fear or resentment..

Clashes with Others

Conflicts with other members of the group. While some conflict may facilitate creativity, too much can keep members from contributing.

POSSIBLE MOTIVATIONS	POSSIBLE ACTIONS FOR LEADER AND/OR OTHERS

* *Does not like one or more group members*
* *Enjoys being divisive*
* *Wishes to hurt or embarrass others*

Standard Procedures/Prevention Strategies

* Focus on group goal or problem to be solved, not on personalities.
* Seat two members known to clash side-by-side, not across from each other.
* Emphasize points of agreement; minimize points of disagreement.

Options for the Current Situation

* Allow clashing individuals to share feelings with one another or with the whole group.
* Brainstorm alternative suggestions for dealing with the issue that has stimulated the clash, allowing group to focus on goal.
* Invite an objective member to talk.
* Emphasize common goal and ask how each relates to it.
* Request that member(s) stop arguing.
* Give an "I" message, e.g., "I feel very disappointed when I hear such biting remarks."

Energetic Considerations

* Soften the energy field by envisioning soft colors, such as pink and light green.

Dominates

Talks a lot, taking control of the group. May be bossy or arrogant, although not necessarily.

POSSIBLE MOTIVATIONS	POSSIBLE ACTIONS FOR LEADER AND/OR OTHERS

POSSIBLE MOTIVATIONS

- *Is eager*
- *Likes showing off*
- *Enjoys being center of attention*
- *Prefers to be in charge*
- *Is exceptionally well informed and anxious to share information*
- *Is naturally garrulous*
- *Displays enthusiasm by talking*

POSSIBLE ACTIONS FOR LEADER AND/OR OTHERS

Standard Procedures/Prevention Strategies

- Arrange for everyone to contribute; proper structuring can curtail long-winded persons.
- Develop new ground rules (or remind group of existing ground rules).
- Set an intention for the group, such as, "open communications and constructive actions."

Options for the Current Situation

- Ask the group to respond to the one who is dominating, "What do some of you think (or feel) about what _____ has just said?"
- Interrupt, emphasizing task and time.
- Say, "That's an interesting point. Let's see what others in the group think about it."
- Use the individual for summarizing, with the expectation that the individual will need to listen to others in order to summarize.
- Ask, without blaming, "What's the intention?"

Energetic Considerations

- Assist the person to be empowered from the inside so that he or she will not have to take power from others in the group.

Refuses to Budge from Position

Exhibits stubborn behavior, related to the group or individuals or with respect to the issues under consideration.

POSSIBLE MOTIVATIONS	POSSIBLE ACTIONS FOR LEADER AND/OR OTHERS

POSSIBLE MOTIVATIONS

- *Does not want to change a prejudgment*
- *Has little or no identity with group goal*
- *Feels ownership of an idea or project not felt by the group*
- *Misunderstands or did not hear others*
- *Is frustrated*
- *Is naturally stubborn*
- *Does not feel part of the group*
- *Has not had an opportunity to explain reasons*
- *Does not feel heard*

POSSIBLE ACTIONS FOR LEADER AND/OR OTHERS

Standard Procedures/Prevention Strategies

- Search for solutions acceptable to all, using problem-solving methods and consensus.
- Trust the group process to eliminate ideas that are not valuable to pursue.

Options for the Current Situation

- Be certain individual is heard.
- Do not argue.
- Break group into smaller groups to generate ideas, refocusing the energy.
- State that group must make decisions. Set a time limit on discussion, then insist the idea die.
- Say that you will discuss it later, if this is true.
- Ask individual to accept group viewpoint for the moment; later there may be time to explore his or her viewpoint more fully.
- Ask the group as a whole to consider and state group's and/or members' intention.

Energetic Considerations

- Imagine the individual encircled with golden light, free from fear and frustration.

Behavior Patterns
that are
Off the Topic

Behavior that takes the group away from the topic or goal can be dysfunctional. Naturally, interesting stories and enriching humor can help to lighten the load of responsibility. A group that is not task-oriented enough can frustrate those who value goals and accomplishments; a group that is *too* task-oriented can lack spontaneity and joy.

Individual group members have different levels of tolerance for diversions and digressions. Leaders can use certain key members in the group as barometers to test the tolerance level.

Some individuals move off course regularly. As soon as they begin to speak, others at the meeting may disengage their attention. Visual cues are eyes turn to papers on the table or friends nod knowingly to each other or someone has to leave the room, ostensibly to go to the rest room or make an important telephone call.

These cues are helpful to notice. In addition, something is happening in the energy field. Group members sensitive to energy or energetics notice immediately when an individual's or the group's attention is lost. It is important to stop the off-the-topic behavior *before* the attention is lost, whenever possible. If that is not possible, stopping this behavior *when* the attention is lost is essential. Specific suggestions for energy balancing are noted in the different patterns that follow.

Some off-the-topic behavior is carelessness within the range of normal human behavior, which can easily be corrected with simple, kind statements. Deeply ingrained off-the-topic behavior can be more difficult to manage. Kindness is still in order, but direct confrontation must be used if the group's progress is truly threatened. It is one thing to spend energy on constructive tasks, and quite another to have energy drained by meaningless chatter and frustration.

Asks Frequent or Irrelevant Questions

Asks questions that seem to be off the subject and/or asks questions more often than seems normal.

POSSIBLE MOTIVATIONS	POSSIBLE ACTIONS FOR LEADER AND/OR OTHERS
• *Is curious* • *Has experience with similar situation and wants to help this group keep out of trouble* • *Wants to be center of attention* • *Is not paying attention* • *Wants to slow or stop group progress* • *Is afraid of not understanding*	**Standard Procedures/Prevention Strategies** • Suggest, "Let's take a few moments to all think quietly about this issue before discussing it (or before asking questions about it)." • Say to the group, "Please hold questions until _____" on the assumption that most questions will be answered during that time. **Options for the Current Situation** • Thank the individual who persistently asks questions and then ask if others have questions. • Give the individual a job (e.g., taking minutes or recording ideas on newsprint.) • Ask if others have questions. If others appear to have something to say, call them by name. • Say, "I'd like to hear from some of you who have not yet spoken." • Say directly to the individual, "When you ask so many (or such) questions, I wonder if you're listening to what we've already said." **Energetic Considerations** • Envision clear energy dropping into the mental aspect of the person.

Digresses

Deviates from the main subject. The one who wanders from the topic may find it difficult to recognize this behavior as a digression.

POSSIBLE MOTIVATIONS	POSSIBLE ACTIONS FOR LEADER AND/OR OTHERS
• *Misunderstands task* • *Seems or is preoccupied with another issue* • *Enjoys being center of attention* • *Has an interesting story to tell*	**Standard Procedures/Prevention Strategies** • Clarify agenda items and direct the group. • Use a flip chart or chalk board to identify current subject. **Options for the Current Situation** • Accept responsibility. "Perhaps I was unclear." • Acknowledge that the individual's topic is important and can be discussed at another time. (Specify time, if at all possible.) • Remind individual that "We really *must* stay on track," if he or she persists. • Listen to find a way to connect digression with agenda item. • Identify participant's contributions as digression, if the behavior pattern continues. • Coach the individual on a one-to-one basis, offering constructive ideas for organizing thoughts or making reports. • Enjoy the story. **Energetic Considerations** • Hold an intention for focused energy.

Discusses Wrong Topic

Talks about a subject other than the one on which the group is scheduled to be focused.

POSSIBLE MOTIVATIONS	POSSIBLE ACTIONS FOR LEADER AND/OR OTHERS

POSSIBLE MOTIVATIONS

- *Misunderstands the topic or assignment*
- *Did not hear the agenda item*
- *Is not paying attention*
- *Seems or is preoccupied with another topic*
- *Is enthusiastic about another issue*

POSSIBLE ACTIONS FOR LEADER AND/OR OTHERS

Standard Procedures/Prevention Strategies

- Write topic or agenda on newsprint, chalkboard, or individual sheets.
- Summarize from time to time, relating to proper topic.

Options for the Current Situation

- Accept responsibility: "Something I said must have led us off the topic; let's return to ____."
- Remind individual or group as a whole of the proper topic.
- Mention when the individual's topic can or will be discussed, if appropriate.
- Use humor that acknowledges topic is incorrect without "putting down" the individual.
- Interrupt and reclarify the topic.
- Stop the group process with a non-blaming question: "Let's check where we are now. Are we discussing _____?"

Energetic Considerations

- Picture in your mind the group participants in synergistic discussion about the appropriate topic.

Makes Wrong or Inappropriate Remarks

Makes comments that do not fit the subject or that are factually incorrect.

POSSIBLE MOTIVATIONS	POSSIBLE ACTIONS FOR LEADER AND/OR OTHERS

POSSIBLE MOTIVATIONS

- *Has not heard previous discussion*
- *Misunderstands agenda or others' remarks*
- *Is unprepared*
- *Is misinformed*
- *Is illogical*
- *Is preoccupied with another issue*

POSSIBLE ACTIONS FOR LEADER AND/OR OTHERS

Standard Procedures/Prevention Strategies

- Establish that it is o.k. to be wrong; avoid harsh reactions when someone makes a mistake.
- Admit your own mistakes, directly and gently, then move on to next matter.

Options for the Current Situation

- Handle with care. Everyone makes mistakes. Model compassion and directness.
- Say, "Let's check the facts."
- Respond, "That's a possibility." Or, "That's one way of looking at it." Ask for other suggestions from the group or offer your own.
- Comment, "I see your point. How can we equate that with this?"
- Be honest and say, "I'm not certain how that relates to this." Or, "I don't agree."
- Question the person. You may find a connection.
- Ignore the misstatement; there may be no point to drawing attention to it.

Energetic Considerations

- Envision the mission of the group as a sphere which moves into the center of the meeting.

Rambles

Talks at random, drifting and straying, usually over several different topics.

POSSIBLE MOTIVATIONS	POSSIBLE ACTIONS FOR LEADER AND/OR OTHERS

POSSIBLE MOTIVATIONS

- *Is preoccupied with own interests*
- *Is unaware of or uninterested in group goal*
- *Misunderstands group goal*
- *Likes to talk*
- *Is disorganized*
- *Needs time to get to the point*

Standard Procedures/Prevention Strategies

- Set group goals initially; restate them to keep everyone, especially the one who rambles, on target.
- Set a standard of limiting comments to, say, two minutes.

Options for the Current Situation

- Thank individual and focus attention by restating relevant points. Move on to another individual.
- Remind individual and group as a whole of realistic and fair time constraints.
- Question the one who is rambling, directing her or him to the subject and task.
- Emphasize time, task, and structure.
- Acknowledge valid points so that the person knows he or she is heard.

Energetic Considerations

- Notice the energy of the group; if it is toxic or heavy or scattered, envision the energy moving around the room in a clockwise direction, especially at eye level.

Behavior Patterns
that
Slow or Depress Progress

The primary purpose for individuals to come together in meetings is to accomplish something they cannot accomplish alone. The synergy of meetings can be exhilarating. Behavior that inhibits this flow of energy can be counterproductive. Such behavior is particularly frustrating to those who value the group process. Movement of thoughts and energy and the process is everyone's responsibility.

Sometimes behavior that slows down the group may be the strategy that serves the highest good. Exciting discussions need to be balanced with reflection or breaks. Meetings that are *too* fast-paced can railroad decisions or slide into obvious solutions when deeper ones are needed.

Some individuals regularly slow down progress. Some groups regularly get bogged down. When groups need to make a decision and cannot because of ineffective behavior or because they do not know how to respond to ineffective behavior, they are unable to fulfill their mission. Blaming often follows. Effective members are likely to find other ways to spend their time, if they have such a choice.

Those who slow down or depress progress are often unfulfilled in their life or in their participation with the group. Such behavior is as loud a communication as the more aggressive and attacking behavior discussed earlier.

Leaders and participants who observe behavior that slows down the group process may find that the best strategy is compassion. Compassion is an energy that can envelop and uplift those who are disempowered or annoyed or unhappy.

Blocks Group Process

Slows down or stops the progress of the group by saying or not saying certain things.

POSSIBLE MOTIVATIONS	POSSIBLE ACTIONS FOR LEADER AND/OR OTHERS
• *Does not feel a commitment to the group or the current subject* • *Expects group to take a course of action contrary to individual's desires or opinions* • *Wants more information before proceeding*	**Standard Procedures/Prevention Strategies** • Encourage members to state personal goals for group participation, for a particular project, or for the current meeting. • Lead a group discussion on a regular basis about the satisfaction with group's process. **Options for the Current Situation** • Name the situation as you see it: "Your comments seem to be slowing down the process." Or, "I know that many of you have ideas, yet you're not saying anything. The group cannot proceed if that continues." • Encourage members -- especially those who are known to be fair and direct -- to express their opinions and ideas. **Energetic Considerations** • Notice if the group energy seems blocked. You may intuit or feel that it is blocked. If so, hold an intention that the group be free of blocks or envision the energy moving clockwise around the room. • Remind yourself of the group's mission; envision a circle drawn around the mission.

Complains

Expresses negative feelings, especially of dissatisfaction or resentment. Behavior may include murmurs, whines, grumbles.

POSSIBLE MOTIVATIONS	POSSIBLE ACTIONS FOR LEADER AND/OR OTHERS

*   *Has pet peeve*
*   *Enjoys quarreling*
*   *Is frustrated*
*   *Has legitimate complaint*
*   *Is unhappy about something unrelated to the current situation*

Standard Procedures/Prevention Strategies

*   Listen to what group members have to say as a matter of style.

Options for the Current Situation

*   Let person know that the gripe has been heard (if appropriate, acknowledge agreement without fueling the anger); direct group forward.
*   Acknowledge that you appreciate assessing problems and negative forces; direct group to seek *solutions* to these.
*   Record complaint; assure that it will be considered and/or passed to the appropriate person.
*   Indicate that you will discuss the concern privately, later. (Be certain to follow up.)
*   Check with other group members. If others relate to the complaint, deal with it immediately and constructively; if not, move on.
*   Indicate remaining time must be spent finding solutions or on the next agenda item.

Energetic Considerations

*   Surround the person in white or golden light in your mind's eye or imagination.

Expresses Negative Attitudes

Talks about the dark or negative side of issues, often in a derogatory or demeaning way.

POSSIBLE MOTIVATIONS	POSSIBLE ACTIONS FOR LEADER AND/OR OTHERS

POSSIBLE MOTIVATIONS

- *Is displeased with the current situation*
- *Is generally negative*
- *Has a legitimate complaint*
- *Wants to be center of attention*
- *Disapproves of leadership or how meetings are conducted*
- *Feels frustrated about previous group decisions*

POSSIBLE ACTIONS FOR LEADER AND/OR OTHERS

Standard Procedures/Prevention Strategies

- Keep tone of meeting positive while being open to hearing negative aspects or possible problems so that you do not miss warnings.
- Be solution-oriented.

Options for the Current Situation

- Acknowledge you have heard the observation, then inquire, "What solutions can you suggest?"
- Check with other group members to see if attitude is supported.
- Invite group to discuss or solve the problem.
- Ask, without blaming, that the person consider intention: his, hers, theirs, the group's.
- Say, "That's one perspective, I have a different one (or, does anyone have a different one?)."
- Help member to express clear statements or specific examples, rather than vague, negative generalizations.

Energetic Considerations

- See duality in situations so that you can allow your perception to transcend duality and embrace wholeness.

Holds Side Conversation

Talks with one or more persons during the meeting proceedings, drawing the attention and energy of one or more members.

POSSIBLE MOTIVATIONS	POSSIBLE ACTIONS FOR LEADER AND/OR OTHERS

POSSIBLE MOTIVATIONS

- *Finds session unresponsive to personal needs*
- *Is uncomfortable talking to entire group*
- *Wants to catch up on other information*
- *Needs to inform someone about an important matter*
- *Is bored*

POSSIBLE ACTIONS FOR LEADER AND/OR OTHERS

Standard Procedures/Prevention Strategies

- Establish a member-agreed policy (a ground rule or norm) that only one person talk at a time when the group is in session.

- Suggest that members write notes to each other so conversations will not distract others.

- Rearrange seating to move known side-talkers away from each other.

Options for the Current Situation

- Comment that you find it is more satisfactory if only one person talks at a time.

- Suggest "buzz" groups (See Chapter 7).

- Assume conversation is important. "We all want to hear what everyone is saying."

- Stand near those who are talking.

- Stop talking. Side-talkers will feel exposed. When they stop their conversation, continue.

- Call one side-talker by name, asking an easy question. Avoid embarrassing the offenders.

Energetic Considerations

- Imagine pure light energy is moving into the group from everyone's higher consciousness.

Requests Leader's Opinion

Asks leader to take a stand on issues by expressing a position, belief, or conviction.

POSSIBLE MOTIVATIONS	POSSIBLE ACTIONS FOR LEADER AND/OR OTHERS

POSSIBLE MOTIVATIONS

- *Attempts to get leader to support one side*
- *Wants to put leader on the spot*
- *Respects leader's opinion and wants to hear it*
- *Is simply looking for leader's direction or advice*

POSSIBLE ACTIONS FOR LEADER AND/OR OTHERS

Standard Procedures/Prevention Strategies

- Clarify leader's role initially: chair, president, facilitator, manager, trainer, consultant, or other. Restate this, if necessary.
- Avoid taking sides, especially in controversial issues.
- Allow group to make its own decisions with the leader's help.

Options for the Current Situation

- Acknowledge that your personal view is relatively unimportant compared to views of group members in total.
- Delay giving an answer. "First let's hear other opinions." Or, "I feel it is inappropriate to give my personal opinion at this time."
- Defer to group, "Let's hear what group members have to say."
- Give a direct answer; there are times when the leader's opinion is important.

Energetic Considerations

- Hold a vision of the leader supporting the group with a non-anxious presence.

Responds Too Quickly

Responds so rapidly that others do not have an opportunity to participate.

POSSIBLE MOTIVATIONS	POSSIBLE ACTIONS FOR LEADER AND/OR OTHERS

POSSIBLE MOTIVATIONS

- *Wants to be helpful*
- *Knows the answers and wants to express them*
- *May or may not want to exclude others from participating; result is the same*
- *Is energized by his or her own participation*

POSSIBLE ACTIONS FOR LEADER AND/OR OTHERS

Standard Procedures/Prevention Strategies

- Suggest, "Let's take a few moments to all think quietly before discussing this."
- Give the individual a job (e.g., taking minutes, recording ideas on newsprint, or summarizing).
- Form small groups when you want the input of many. Comments that follow are likely to be of higher quality than initial quick ones.
- Introduce centering. (See Chapter 7.)

Options for the Current Situation

- Thank the individual and ask group if others would like to participate.
- Question others you know have information.
- Give others an invitation to speak, "I'd like to hear from those who have not yet spoken."
- Tease the individual gently, noting how quick he or she is.
- Say directly, "When you respond so quickly, others don't have a chance to participate."

Energetic Considerations

- Direct energy from the higher selves to each one in the group.

Uses Unkind Humor

Uses put-downs, such as racial or ethnic or sexist comments, intending or believing the comment is funny.

POSSIBLE MOTIVATIONS	POSSIBLE ACTIONS FOR LEADER AND/OR OTHERS

POSSIBLE MOTIVATIONS

- *Means to be funny, but results in being mean*
- *Wants to break the ice*
- *Wants to be accepted by a group or person who dislikes the one or ones being slurred*

POSSIBLE ACTIONS FOR LEADER AND/OR OTHERS

Standard Procedures/Prevention Strategies

- Do not laugh at unkind humor. It is not funny. Laughter encourages the put-downs; lack of laughter discourages the put-downs.

- Establish a kindness policy. Unkind actions will not fit; they will stop or will not start.

- Read humorous book passages or antidotes that enrich and empower individuals, providing a model for kind humor.

Options for the Current Situation

- Name what you see. "I hear that as an unkind comment." Or, "I don't consider what you said is funny. In fact, I'm offended by it."

- Use humor to lift up the person or group to whom unkind humor has been directed. If unkind humor is the norm at your meetings, plan responses to be ready for put-downs.

- Remember that not everyone who uses put-down or unkind humor intends to be mean; this behavior is rampant in our culture.

Energetic Considerations

- Encircle everyone involved -- the subject and the object of the unkindness -- in love energy.

Behavior Patterns
That
Hide Information

Sharing information is a primary purpose for individuals to hold meetings. Information includes opinions, facts, feelings, accomplishments, fears, and joys. Of course, not all information can be shared. There is not enough time for everyone to talk about everything he or she feels, believes, or knows.

When the group's goal and intention are clear, relevant information is usually obvious to most of those attending. Keeping the group's intention and today's meeting agenda in the forefront helps to remind participants what information is relevant and helps to prevent hiding important information.

Leaders and group members can support the open sharing of information by making the environment safe. When some or many participants attack individuals or ideas, the more timid group members are less likely to offer their contributions. It is important to remember that quiet individuals often have more valuable observations than noisy ones. The quality of information is more important than the volume.

High intentions and empowering affirmations support a group in experiencing open communications. When meetings are conducive to information sharing, the energy flows smoothly and participants are clear whose turn it is to speak. Revelations occur as a matter of course. The movement of energy from one person to the next is effortless, like a dance or a symphony.

Hides a Personal Agenda

Holds an intention, which is kept hidden, to turn the group in a particular direction or to thwart a group decision.

POSSIBLE MOTIVATIONS	POSSIBLE ACTIONS FOR LEADER AND/OR OTHERS

POSSIBLE MOTIVATIONS

- *Wants something different from the stated meeting intent*

- *Wants to do something in addition to the stated meeting intent*

- *Seems or is preoccupied with an issue outside the meeting scope*

- *Misunderstands the purpose of this meeting or group*

- *Wishes to be in control*

- *Has high opinion of group potential and tries to stretch members*

POSSIBLE ACTIONS FOR LEADER AND/OR OTHERS

Standard Procedures/Prevention Strategies

- Encourage members to express personal goals so that irrelevant issues can be identified and passed to appropriate place or person.

- Watch for evidence of personal or secret agenda items; ignore or confront them, as appropriate.

Options for the Current Situation

- Re-focus on the stated agenda if meeting seems to move toward a single individual's purpose.

- Acknowledge that the individual's topic, if revealed, is important and can be discussed at another time. (Specify time, if possible.)

- Ask directly, "What are the hidden agendas today?" if group has a history of operating this way. General awareness will be raised and specific issues may be brought into the open.

Energetic Considerations

- Notice if energy feels tight any place as you circle energy clockwise around the group; if so, state an intention of free-flowing energy and envision the energy loosening.

Says Little or Nothing

Does not speak freely or openly. The person appears to be reserved, uncommunicative, reticent, shy, or quiet.

POSSIBLE MOTIVATIONS

- *Is naturally quiet*
- *Is bored, preoccupied, frustrated, or indifferent*
- *Feels superior*
- *Is timid*
- *Feels shy or uncomfortable with group*
- *Prefers to listen*
- *Is waiting for the "right" moment to speak*
- *Needs time to process information*

POSSIBLE ACTIONS FOR LEADER AND/OR OTHERS

Standard Procedures/Prevention Strategies

- Create a climate that is conducive for all group participants to express themselves. Also, value contributions of all members.

Options for the Current Situation

- Ask, "Is there anyone who wishes to speak who has not had the opportunity?".

- Say to the person, "We want to hear *your* viewpoint, too." Use caution about singling out a timid member; it might create embarrassment.

- Encourage, but do not insist, the person speak. Everyone has the right to participate silently.

- Watch the individual. If he or she takes a breath as if to speak but gets cut off, make an opening by calling him or her by name.

- Make eye contact with the quiet individual; perhaps she or he is processing information and has a contribution that acts as a summary.

- Accept that some persons are naturally quiet.

Energetic Considerations

- Hold a high intention that all individuals speak their truth freely and clearly.

Speaks Inarticulately

Lacks the power or faculty of fluent speech or the ability to be persuasive and forceful.

POSSIBLE MOTIVATIONS

- *Lacks capability to put thoughts into words*
- *Lacks experience putting thoughts into words*
- *Is surrounded by very articulate persons, emphasizing her or his problem*
- *Needs time to process information before speaking or by speaking*
- *Is shy*

POSSIBLE ACTIONS FOR LEADER AND/OR OTHERS

Standard Procedures/Prevention Strategies

- Say regularly to summarize and check meaning, "Let me see if I understand." Then repeat participants' ideas as you understand them.

Options for the Current Situation

- Use patience and good sense. Patience is needed to help the individual express thoughts articulately; good sense, to keep group alert and interested.
- Avoid phrase "What you mean is ...." This can feel demeaning, especially to one who is shy or struggling with self expression.
- Offer to coach the person prior to meeting, especially if he or she has a report to make.
- Give the person time and space. If you and others understand the essence, respond as if the idea were stated clearly. The person's practice and your acceptance may be more important than perfect expression.

Energetic Considerations

- Give compassionate, unfrustrated attention, so that you do not give the energy of annoyance to the one who is already struggling.

Withholds Important Information

Conceals data that is important or potentially important to the group's progress.

POSSIBLE MOTIVATIONS	POSSIBLE ACTIONS FOR LEADER AND/OR OTHERS

POSSIBLE MOTIVATIONS

- *Has a hidden agenda (See earlier in this Chapter)*
- *Is angry at someone*
- *Does not understand that the information is important*
- *Feels that the information will not be welcome, based on history of the group*
- *Feels the pressure of time and so does not offer the information*
- *Does not want to stir up trouble or feelings, etc.*

POSSIBLE ACTIONS FOR LEADER AND/OR OTHERS

Standard Procedures/Prevention Strategies

- Create an atmosphere of safety to encourage information sharing.
- Encourage quiet time (see centering in Chapter 7), so that important matters are more likely to be revealed.
- Brainstorm (see Chapter 7) to list many ideas before spending time on the most obvious ideas.

Options for the Current Situation

- Invite others to express diverse views, "Is there information (or an opinion) that hasn't been stated?" Or, "Is there someone who hasn't had a chance to say something?"
- Accept responsibility if you suspect withheld information, "I wonder if we're rushing through this so fast that we might miss something important."
- Ask directly the person whom you know has important information to speak.

Energetic Considerations

- Sense through your own body if tightness indicates that information is withheld.

Chapter 11

Transforming Difficulty into Empowerment

Using Difficulty to Develop

You may wonder why so much attention has been given to difficult behavior in a book called "*Energetic Meetings*." Here is the reason: when we are conscious of the effects of certain actions, we can have mastery over our responses and empower ourselves. Difficult situations teach us that we have choices and help us to clarify what is truly important.

An unfortunate expression is commonly used in our society: "No pain, no gain." I say "unfortunate" because it is an untrue statement, yet many persons believe it is true. And, indeed, some persons believe the expression so much that they *make* it true. Our beliefs provide windows for seeing the world; our beliefs flow into actions.

Our personal histories might substantiate the "No pain, no gain" myth. Most of us have learned from painful experiences. Most of us have acquired deep, meaningful insights after being fired or demoted or embarrassed publically, or after the death of a relationship or betrayal or other emotional pain. So, of course, we *can* gain from pain. We can and do learn from adversity. But it is an unfortunate leap to affirm that the *only* way we can gain is with pain!

If you say, or agree when others say, the expression "No pain, no gain," you may want to ask yourself a question, "Do I want to make pain a prerequisite for gain?" If not, eradicate this expression from your thought patterns and do not collude when others use it. You can replace this disempowering expression with one of many empowering affirmations.

Here are several empowering affirmations* to replace disempowering affirmations that you may be saying to yourself consciously or unconsciously about learning or growing.

> *I love learning.*
>
> *I grow with pleasure.*
>
> *I give myself permission to learn with joy.*
>
> *Every act is an act of empowerment.*
>
> *I am ready for change.*
>
> *As I go through experiences, I grow through experiences.*
>
> *I love change.*
>
> *I give up struggle.*
>
> *I choose freely.*
>
> *I let every situation teach me joyfully.*
>
> *Life is a series of opportunities to choose how to frame the pictures I see.*
>
> *I seek opportunities to let go of outdated beliefs and disempowering ideas.*
>
> *I receive the gifts of life.*

* From *Affirmations: A Pathway to Empowerment* by Jeanie Marshall

The Gifts of Difficult Behavior

Gifts of growth come in many packages. Some are covered with seriousness, some with humor. Some are wrapped in silence, others in conversations. Some are tied with multicolored ribbons of truth and nontruth twisted together. Some are boxed with limitation or frustration, others with wisdom of great sages. Most gifts are hidden right under our noses, just waiting for us to find and open.

Rarely do the individuals who have the greatest gifts for us stand at our doorway handing us a beautifully-wrapped box with a pretty ribbon and a sweet gift card. Our greatest gifts often come from or through those who challenge us the most. The gift may arrive after a stinging comment or a public humiliation or a confrontation with a difficult situation at a meeting. Be as a child: ask that the gift be unwrapped (revealed) as soon as possible.

What are the gifts in *your* life? Or if that question is too big, what are the gifts of yesterday? Or the gifts of the last meeting you attended? Or the gifts of a particular relationship, whether comfortable or uncomfortable? And what are the gifts that you, in turn, give to the world? Gift giving/receiving is a continuous process. Consider your gifts and remember to give thanks for them.

New Paradigm

New paradigms develop because old paradigms no longer work. Meetings have a poor reputation in most settings. "Boring," "deadly," "waste of time," and "unnecessary" are just a few of many common qualifiers often used to describe meetings.

In the old paradigm, meetings have often been used to control information and/or people. Often leaders -- and most often our most competent and exceptionally gifted leaders -- are assaulted in some way. Participants compete, leading to an imbalance of power and no true empowerment. It is time for the New Paradigm.

When a group of people
Come together in a circle with high intention,
Miracles happen.

We
Collaborate
Experience abundance and creativity and energy
Respect one another
Let every situation be an opportunity for empowerment
Relate to others honestly and compassionately
Trust intuitive insights
Know what is worthy of our attention
Recognize that we are part of an interconnected whole.

This is the New Meeting Paradigm.

Books for Further Reading

Here are a few of the many books that are appropriate for follow up to the ideas in *Energtic Meetings*.

New Ways of Being; New Ways of Doing

Barker, Joel Arthur. *Future Edge: Discovering the New Paradigms of Success.* New York: William Morrow and Company, Inc., 1992.

Block, Peter. *The Empowered Manager.* San Francisco, CA: Jossey - Bass Publishers, 1987.

Capra, Fritjof. *The Tao of Physics: An Explanation of the Parallels between Modern Physics and Eastern Mysticism.* Shambhala, 1983.

Costello, Sheila J. *Managing Change in the Workplace.* Boston, MA: Mirror Press, 1994.

Covey, Stephen R. *The Seven Habits of Highly Effective People: Restoring the Character Ethic.* New York: Simon and Schuster, 1989.

Davidson, Gordon and Corrine McLaughlin. *Spiritual Politics: Changing the World from the Inside Out.* New York: Ballatine Books, 1994.

Frieman, Norman. *Bridging Science and Spirit.* St. Louis, MO: Living Lake Books, 1994.

Gleick, James. *Chaos: Making a New Science.* New York: Viking, 1987.

Harman, Willis. *Global Mind Change: The Promise of the Last Years of the Twentieth Century.* Knowledge Systems, 1991.

Hickman, Craig R.; and Silva, Michael A. *Creating Excellence: Managing Corporate Culture, Strategy, and Change in the New Age.* New York: New American Library, 1984.

Koestenbaum, Peter. *The Heart of Business.* Dallas, TX: Saybrook Publishing Co., 1987.

Marshall, Jeanie. *Affirmations: A Pathway to Empowerment.* Santa Monica:, CA. Jemel Publishing House, Publication forthcoming, 1995.

Orsborn, Carol. *Inner Excellence: Spiritual Principles of Life-Driven Business.* San Rafael, CA: New World Library, 1992.

Owen, Harrison. *Spirit: Transformation and Development in Organizations.* Potomac, MD: Abbott Publishing, 1988.

Ray, Michael and Alan Rinzler for the World Business Academy, ed. *The New Paradigm in Business.* New York: G.P. Putnam's Sons, 1993.

Senge, Peter. *The Fifth Discipline: The Art and Practice of the Learning Organization.* New York: Doubleday/Currency, 1990.

Toms. Michael. *At the Leading Edge.* Burdett, NY: Karson Publications, 1991.

Vaill, Peter B. *Managing as a Performing Art: New Ideas for a World of Chaotic Change.* San Francisco, CA: Jossey-Bass Publishers, 1991.

Wheatley, Margaret J. *Leadership and the New Science: Learning about Organization from an Orderly Universe.* San Francisco, CA: Berrett-Koehler Publishers, 1992.

Zukav, Gary. *The Seat of the Soul.* New York: Simon and Schuster, 1989.

Energy, Energy Field, Energetics; Healing

Borysenko, Joan, Ph.D. *Minding the Body, Mending the Mind.* Reading, MA: Addison-Wesley Publishing, 1987.

Brennan, Barbara Ann. *Hands of Light: A Guide to Healing Through the Human Energy Field.* New York: Pleiades Books, 1987.

Crum, Thomas F. *The Magic of Conflict*. New York: Simon and Schuster, 1987.

Chopra, Deepak. *Quantum Healing: Exploring the Frontiers of Mind/Body Medicine*. New York: Bantam Books, 1990.

Davidson, John. *Subtle Energy*. Cambridge, England: Saffron Walden, 1987.

Gerber, Richard. *Vibrational Medicine: New Choices for Healing Ourselves*. Santa Fe, NM: Bear & Company, 1988.

Griscolm, Chris. *Ecstasy is a New Frequency: Teachings of the Light Institute*. Santa Fe, NM: Bear and Company, 1987.

Janiger, Oscar, M.D., and Philip Goldberg. *A Different Kind of Healing*. New York: G.P. Purnam's Sons, 1993.

Marshall, Jeanie. *Symbolic Language of Energy*. Santa Monica, CA: Jemel Publishing House, publication forthcoming (1995).

Sinetar, Marsha. *Elegant Choices, Healing Choices*. Paulist Press, 1989.

Small, Jacquelyn. *Transformers: The Therapists of the Future*. Marina del Rey, CA: DeVorss & company, 1982.

Meetings and Meeting Effectiveness

Bradford, Leland. *Making Meetings Work: A Guide for Leaders and Group Members*. New York: Amacom, 1986.

Doyle, Michael, and Straus, David. *How to Make Meetings Work: The New Interaction Method.* New York: Wyden Books, 1993.

Kieffer, George David. *The Strategy of Meetings*. New York: Simon and Schuster, 1988.

Kirkpatrick, Donald L. *How to Plan and Conduct Productive Business Meetings*. Chicago, IL: The Dartnell Corporation, 1976.

Marshall, Jeanie. *Handling Difficult Behavior at Meetings*. Santa Monica, CA: Marshall House, 1994.

Groups and Group Development

Kolb, David A.; and Fry, Ronald. "Towards an Applied Theory of Experiential Learning." *Theories of Group Processes.* Edited by Cary L. Cooper. London, England: John Wiley & Sons, 1975.

Miles, Matthew B. *Learning to Work in Groups.* New York: Columbia College, 1959.

Schul, Bill D. *How to Be an Effective Group Leader.* Chicago, IL: Nelson-Hall, 1975.

Schutz, William C. *Here Comes Everybody.* New York: Harper & Row, 1971.

Shonk, James H. *Working in Teams: A Practical Manual for Improving Work Groups.* New York: Amacom, 1982.

Simpson, Donald T. "Handling Group and Organizational Conflict," *The 1977 Annual Handbook for Group Facilitators,* John E. Jones, Ph.D., and J. William Pfeifer, Ph.D., ed. La Jolla, CA: University Associates, 1977.

Tuckman, B.W. "Developmental Sequence in Small Groups." *Psychological Bulletin,* 1965, 63, 284-399.

Weber, Richard C. "The Group: A Cycle from Birth to Death." *Reading Book for Human Relations Training,* Lawrence Porter and Bernard Mohr, ed. Arlington, VA: NTL Institute, 1982.

To Order *Energetic Meetings*

$11.00 U.S.   ISBN: 1-885893-00-0

For Visa and MasterCard, call Toll-free, 1-800-460-5855.

For check or money order, payable to Publication Services, Inc., 8870 Business Park Drive, Austin, Texas 78759. (512) 795-5006. Please be certain to include postage and handling charges and applicable sales tax. Checks and money orders must be in U.S. funds drawn on a U.S. bank.

For corporations, book distributors, and book stores, to arrange for quantity discounts, please call Marshall House at (310) 458-1172.

Postage and handling, etc., U.S. $3.00; Canada, $4.00; Overseas $8.00; plus $1.50 for each additional book sent to the same address.

California residents pay sales tax.

Allow four weeks for delivery; faster delivery options are available.

Other Marshall House and Jemel Publishing House publications

For the following items, please contact Marshall House, P.O. Box 918, Santa Monica, CA 90406; Telephone, (310) 458-1172; Fax, (310) 451-2265.

The *Marshall House Journal* is published monthly, except August and December. The *Journal* focuses on empowerment and energetics, especially in the organizational setting. Annual subscription is $30.00; Canadians, please add $3.00; Overseas, please add $10.00.

Handling Difficult Behavior at Meetings by Jeanie Marshall (booklet contains Chapter 10 and other excerpts from *Energetic Meetings*), $5.00 each plus $1.00 for postage and handling; quantity discounts available.

Symbolic Language of Energy by Jeanie Marshall: publication in 1995.

The Marshall House Mailing list alerts you to speaking engagements, services, and publications.

Consulting Services by Jeanie Marshall

To arrange for consulting services for Empowerment and Energetic Clearing, please contact Marshall House, P.O. Box 918, Santa Monica, CA 90406; Telephone, (310) 458-1172; Fax, (310) 451-2265.

Jeanie offers consultations by telephone and audio cassette tape. She also offers an exciting program called, *MAP Energetics*™, which is available in two parts: **The Personal Energetic Clearing Process** and **The Certification Program.**